Trick Geography

USA

STUDENT BOOK

Patty Blackmer

Blackmer Press
Walled Lake, MI

Patty Blackmer holds a Bachelor of Arts degree in English and American Language and Literature and a Master of Arts degree in Secondary School Curriculum with an emphasis in linguistics from Eastern Michigan University. She has taught in both public and private schools. Patty and her husband, Ron, have homeschooled their three sons.

Trick Geography
4425 Newton Rd.
Walled Lake, MI 48390
TrickGeography@outlook.com

Visit our website at:
TrickGeography.com

Copyright © 2016, Patricia Blackmer

All Rights Reserved. No part of this book may be reproduced or utilized in any form or by any means, electronic or mechanical, including photocopying, recording, or by any information storage and retrieval system, without permission in writing from the author.

Thank You!

*Ron and our boys Brendan, Colin, and Grant for years of answering my endless requests
for their opinions;*

*Kate Quinlan for her encouraging words, constructive suggestions,
and for piloting the program;*

*Ellyn Davis at HomeSchoolMarketplace.com for her invaluable advice in helping me
through the publishing process;*

*Tim and Holly Cheyne for their optimism, editing and technical help,
and for getting me across the finish line.*

The Lord bestows on all his own gifts as he doth choose.
It's mine to map his whirling globe and yours to be amused.

P. B.

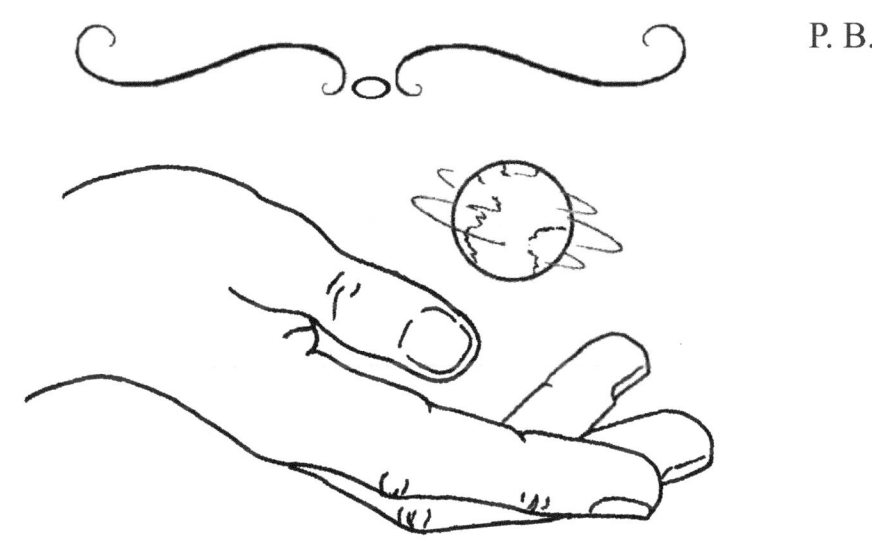

O beautiful for spacious skies,
for amber waves of grain;
for purple mountain majesties
above the fruited plain!
America! America! God shed his grace on thee,
and crown thy good with brotherhood
from sea to shining sea.

—Katharine Lee Bates

Contents

Vocabulary..8

Regions..10

States...11

Capitals..25

Physical Features...39

Tests...45

Where Do We Go From Here?................................55

VOCABULARY

Order of countries and capitals correspond.

STATES

Map 1:
Northeastern
1. Pennsylvania
2. New York
3. Vermont
4. New Hampshire
5. Maine
6. Massachusetts
7. Rhode Island
8. Connecticut
9. New Jersey
10. Delaware
11. Maryland

Map 2:
Southeastern
1. Mississippi
2. Tennessee
3. Kentucky
4. West Virginia
5. Virginia
6. North Carolina
7. South Carolina
8. Georgia
9. Florida
10. Alabama

Map 3: North Central
1. North Dakota
2. South Dakota
3. Minnesota
4. Wisconsin
5. Michigan
6. Ohio
7. Indiana
8. Illinois
9. Iowa
10. Nebraska

Map 4: South Central
1. Oklahoma
2. Kansas
3. Missouri
4. Arkansas
5. Louisiana
6. Texas

Map 5:
Northwestern
1. Alaska
2. Washington
3. Oregon
4. Idaho
5. Wyoming
6. Montana

Map 6:
Southwestern
1. California
2. Nevada
3. Utah
4. Colorado
5. New Mexico
6. Arizona
7. Hawaii

CAPITALS

Map 7:
Northeastern
1. Harrisburg
2. Albany
3. Montpelier
4. Concord
5. Augusta
6. Boston
7. Providence
8. Hartford
9. Trenton
10. Dover
11. Annapolis

Map 8:
Southeastern
1. Jackson
2. Nashville
3. Frankfort
4. Charleston
5. Richmond
6. Raleigh
7. Columbia
8. Atlanta
9. Tallahassee
10. Montgomery

Map 9: North Central
1. Bismarck
2. Pierre
3. St. Paul
4. Madison
5. Lansing
6. Columbus
7. Indianapolis
8. Springfield
9. De Moines
10. Lincoln

Map 10: South Central
1. Oklahoma City
2. Topeka
3. Jefferson City
4. Little Rock
5. Baton Rouge
6. Austin

Map 11:
Northwestern
1. Juneau
2. Olympia
3. Salem
4. Boise
5. Cheyenne
6. Helena

Map 12:
Southwestern
1. Sacramento
2. Carson City
3. Salt Lake City
4. Denver
5. Santa Fe
6. Phoenix
7. Honolulu

 Copyright © 2016, Patricia Blackmer

Map 13: Bodies of Water
1. Yukon River
2. Columbia River
3. Snake River
4. Great Salt Lake
5. Colorado River
6. Rio Grande
7. Mississippi River
8. Missouri River
9. Platte River
10. Arkansas River
11. Red River
12. Ohio River
13. Lake Superior
14. Lake Michigan
15. Lake Huron
16. Lake Erie
17. Lake Ontario

Map 14: Mountains, Deserts, Plains
Mountains
1. Brooks Mountains
2. Alaska Mountains
3. Mount Denali (McKinley)
4. Coastal Mountains
5. Cascade Range
6. Sierra Nevada
7. Mount Whitney
8. Rocky Mountains
9. Mount Elbert
10. Appalachian Mountains
11. Mount Mitchell

Deserts
12. Great Basin Desert
13. Mojave Desert

Plains
14. Great Plains

Copyright © 2016, Patricia Blackmer

UNITED STATES REGIONS

1. Northeastern
2. Southeastern
3. North Central
4. South Central
5. Northwestern
6. Southwestern

Pacific Ocean

Atlantic Ocean

Copyright © 2016, Patricia Blackmer

STATES

MAP 1: NORTHEASTERN STATES

Copyright © 2016, Patricia Blackmer

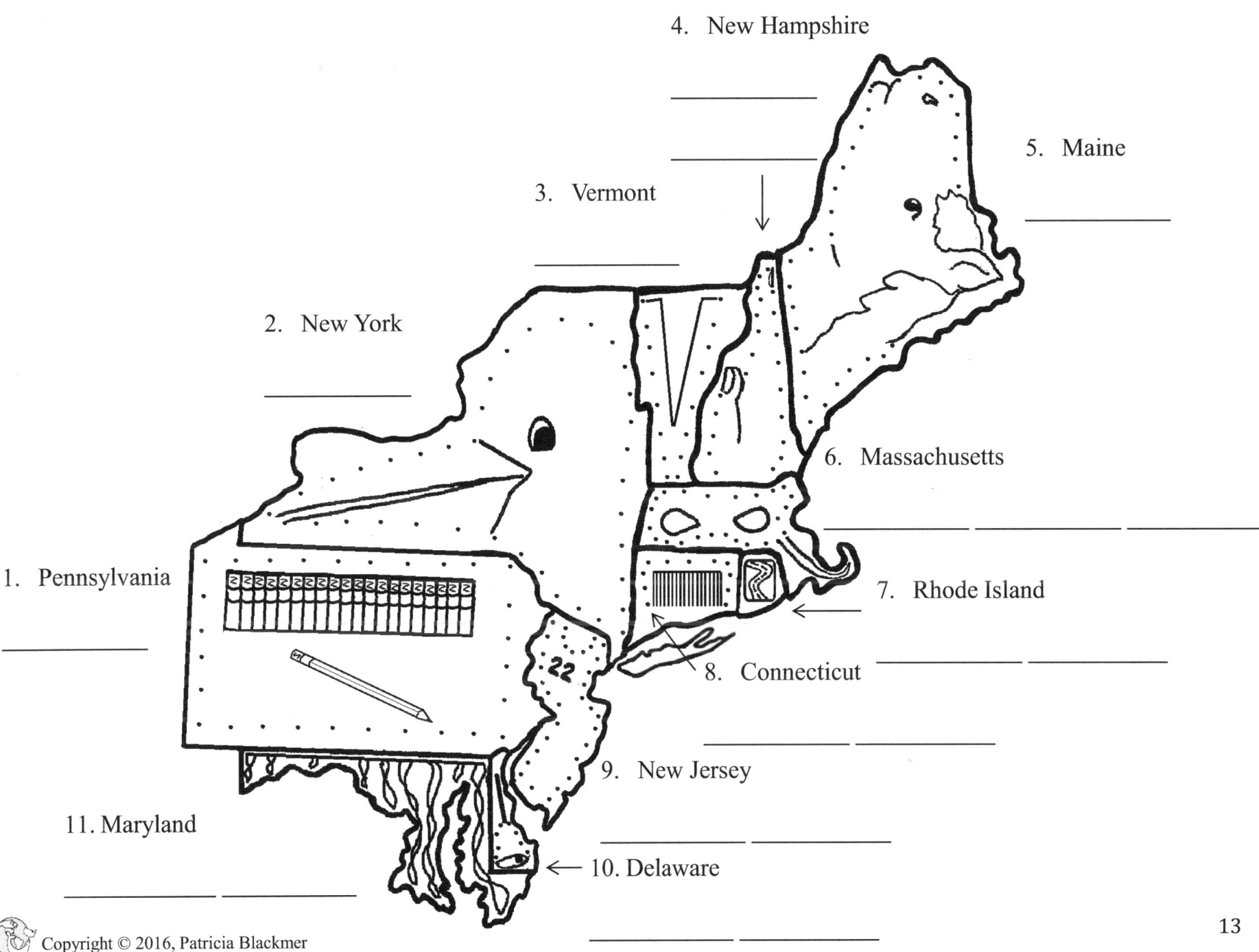

14

MAP 2: SOUTHEASTERN STATES

Copyright © 2016, Patricia Blackmer

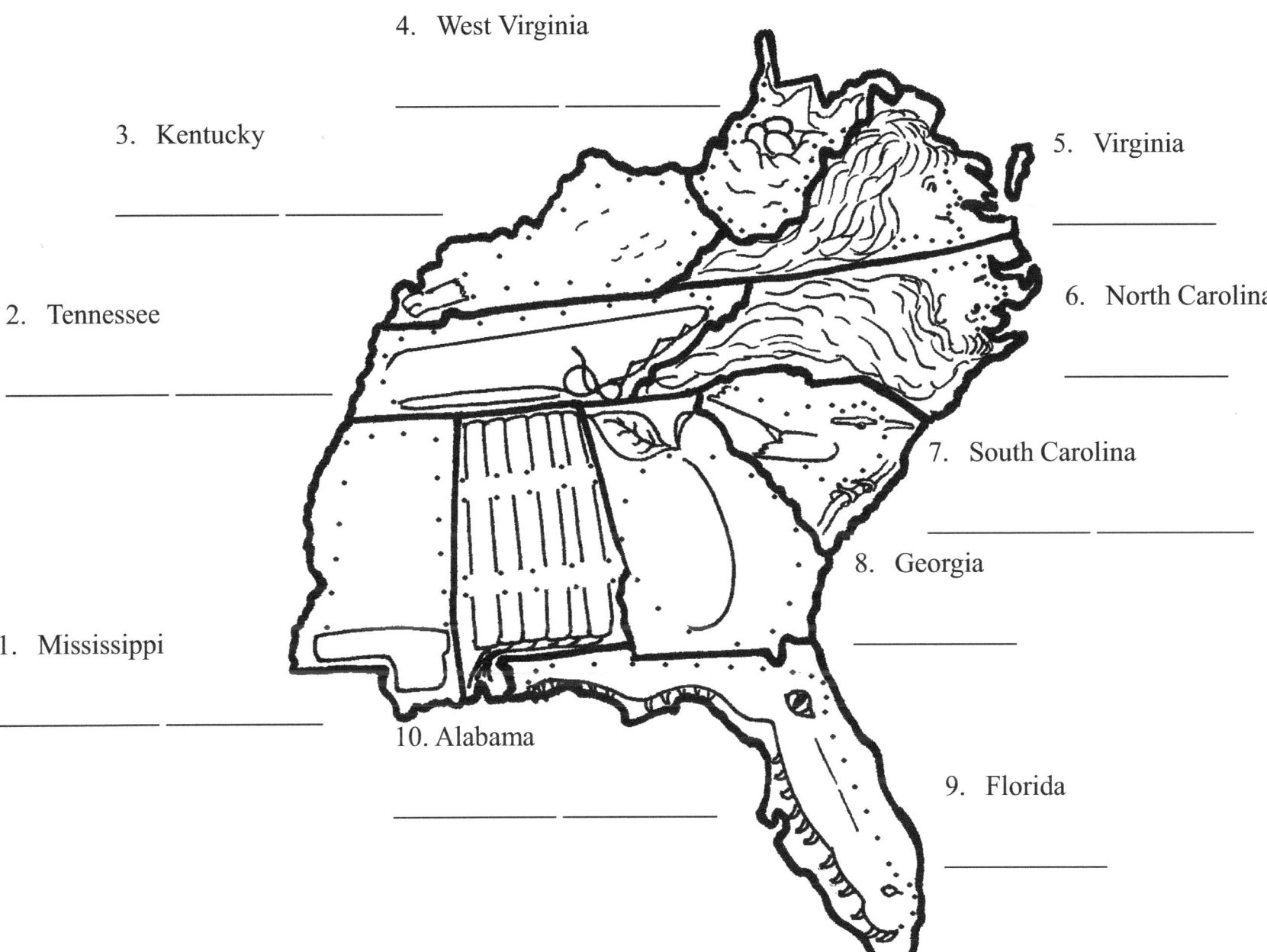

4. West Virginia

3. Kentucky

5. Virginia

2. Tennessee

6. North Carolina

7. South Carolina

8. Georgia

1. Mississippi

10. Alabama

9. Florida

16

MAP 3: NORTH CENTRAL STATES

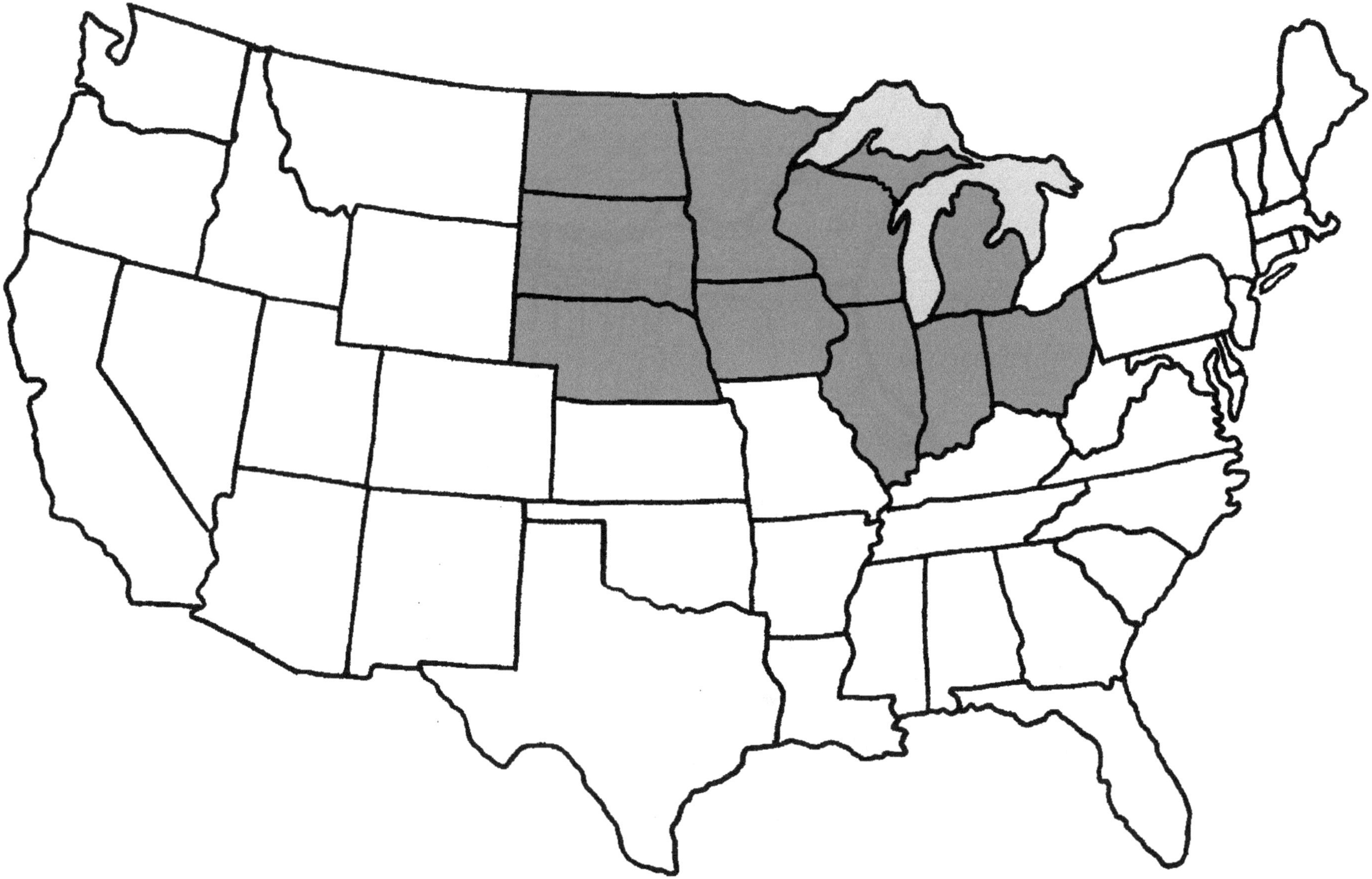

Copyright © 2016, Patricia Blackmer

1. North Dakota
_____

2. South Dakota
_____

3. Minnesota
_____

4. Wisconsin
_____

5. Michigan
_____

6. Ohio
_____

7. Indiana
_____

8. Illinois
_____

9. Iowa
_____

10. Nebraska
_____

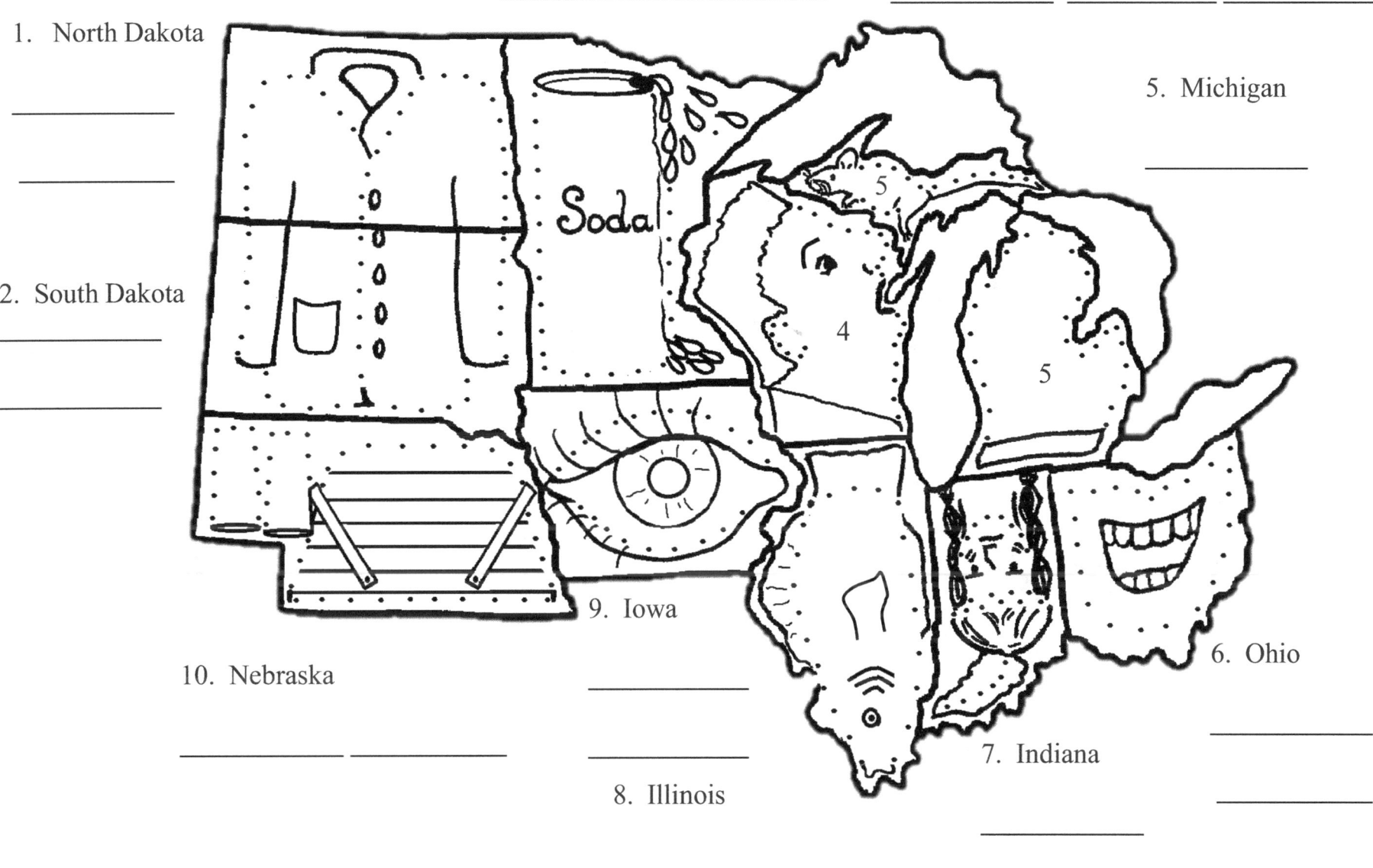

Copyright © 2016, Patricia Blackmer

18

MAP 4: SOUTH CENTRAL STATES

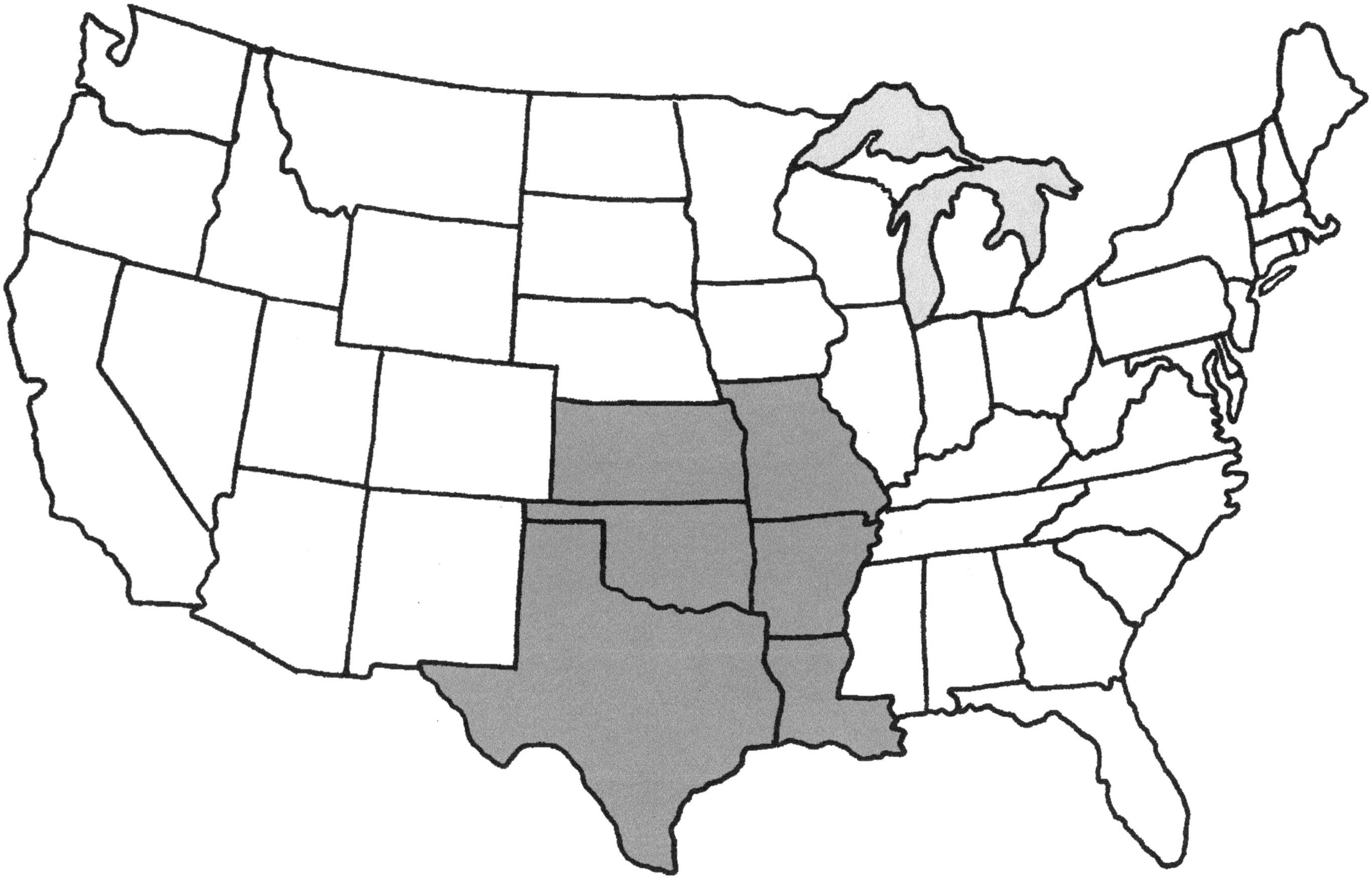

 Copyright © 2016, Patricia Blackmer

1. Oklahoma

2. Kansas

3. Missouri

4. Arkansas

5. Louisiana

6. Texas

20

MAP 5: NORTHWESTERN STATES

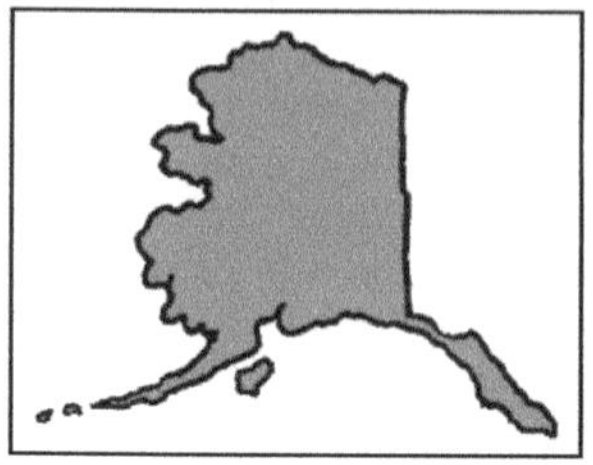

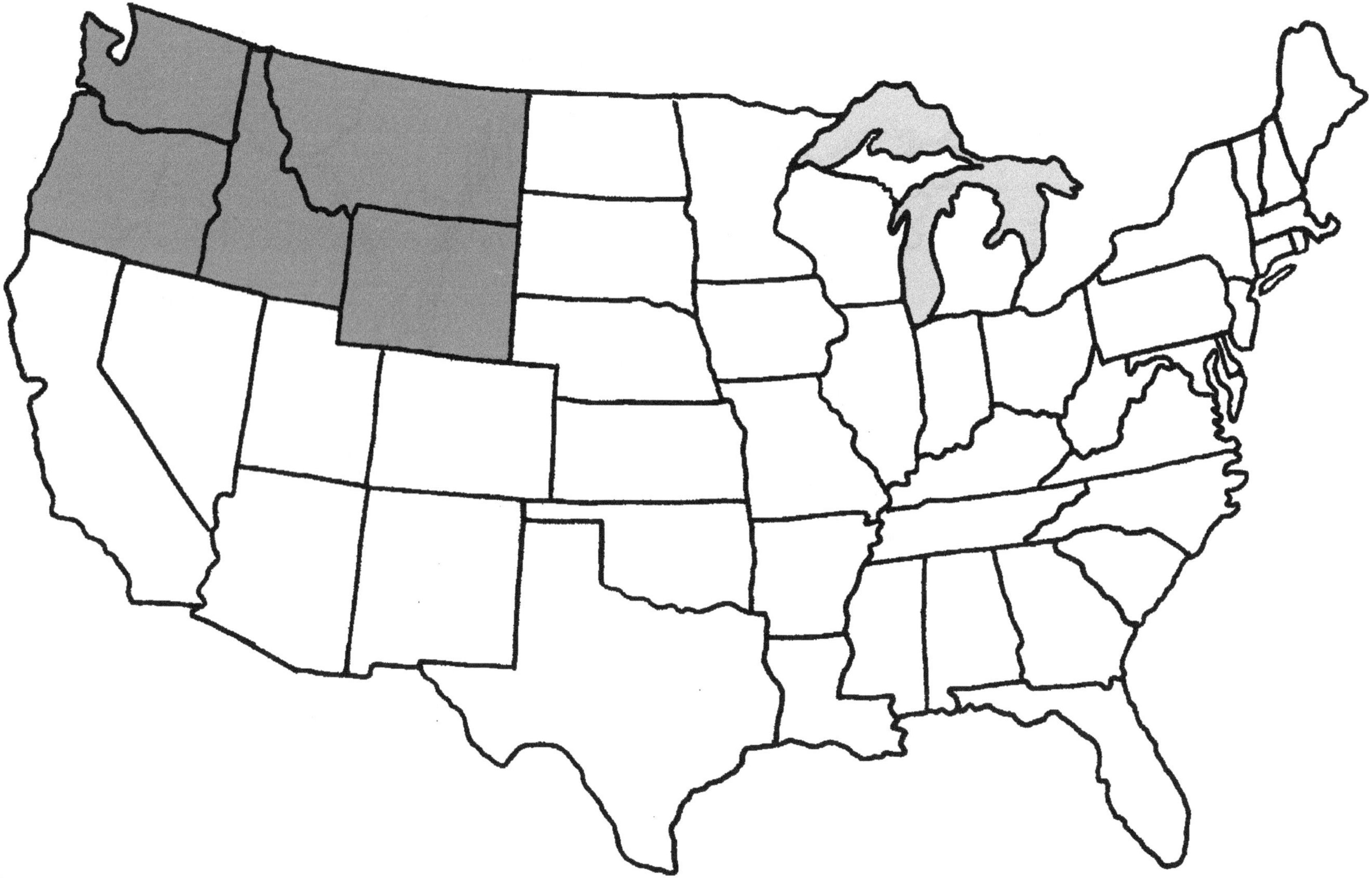

 Copyright © 2016, Patricia Blackmer

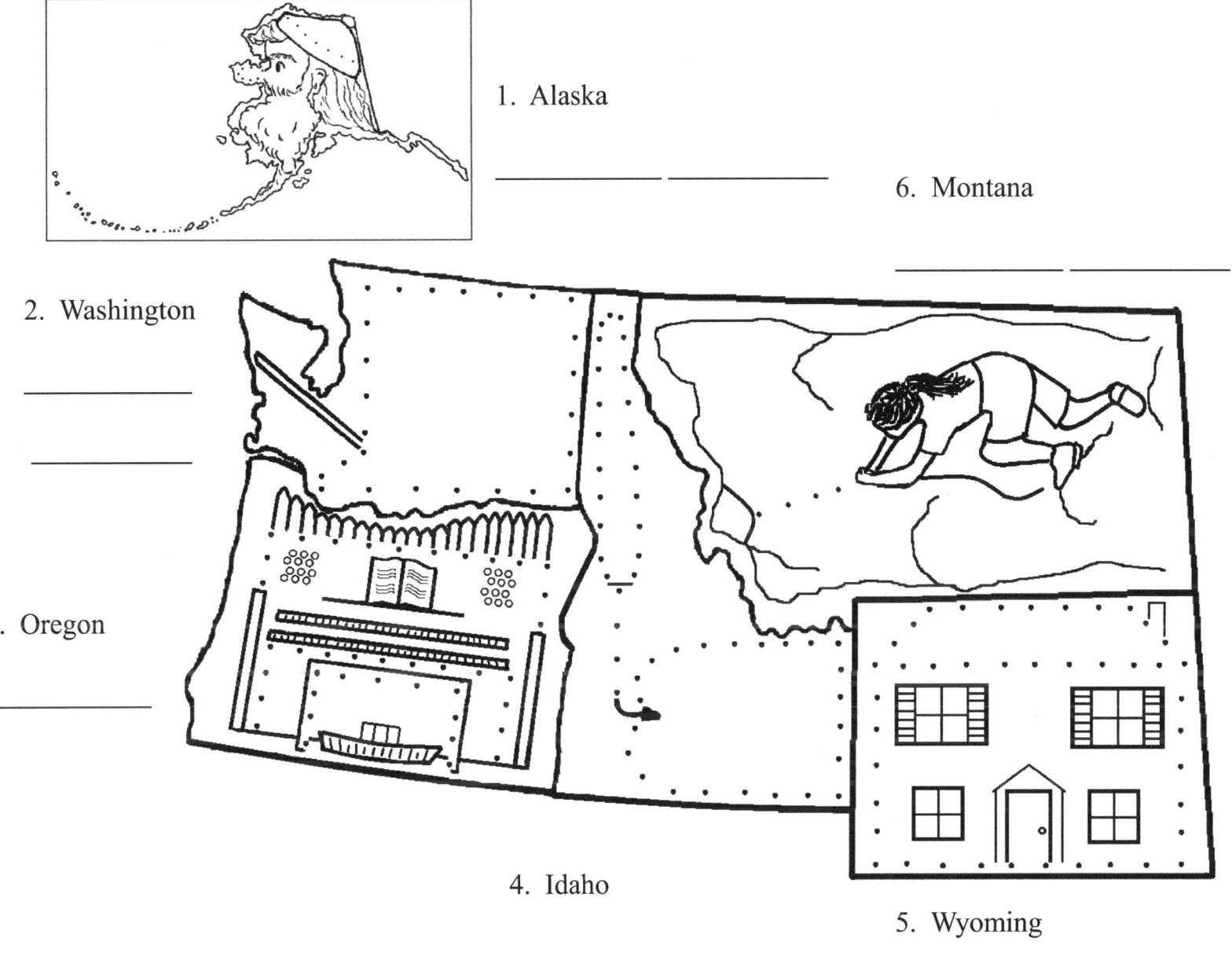

1. Alaska ____ ____

2. Washington ____

3. Oregon ____

4. Idaho ____ ____

5. Wyoming ____ ____

6. Montana ____ ____

22

MAP 6: SOUTHWESTERN STATES

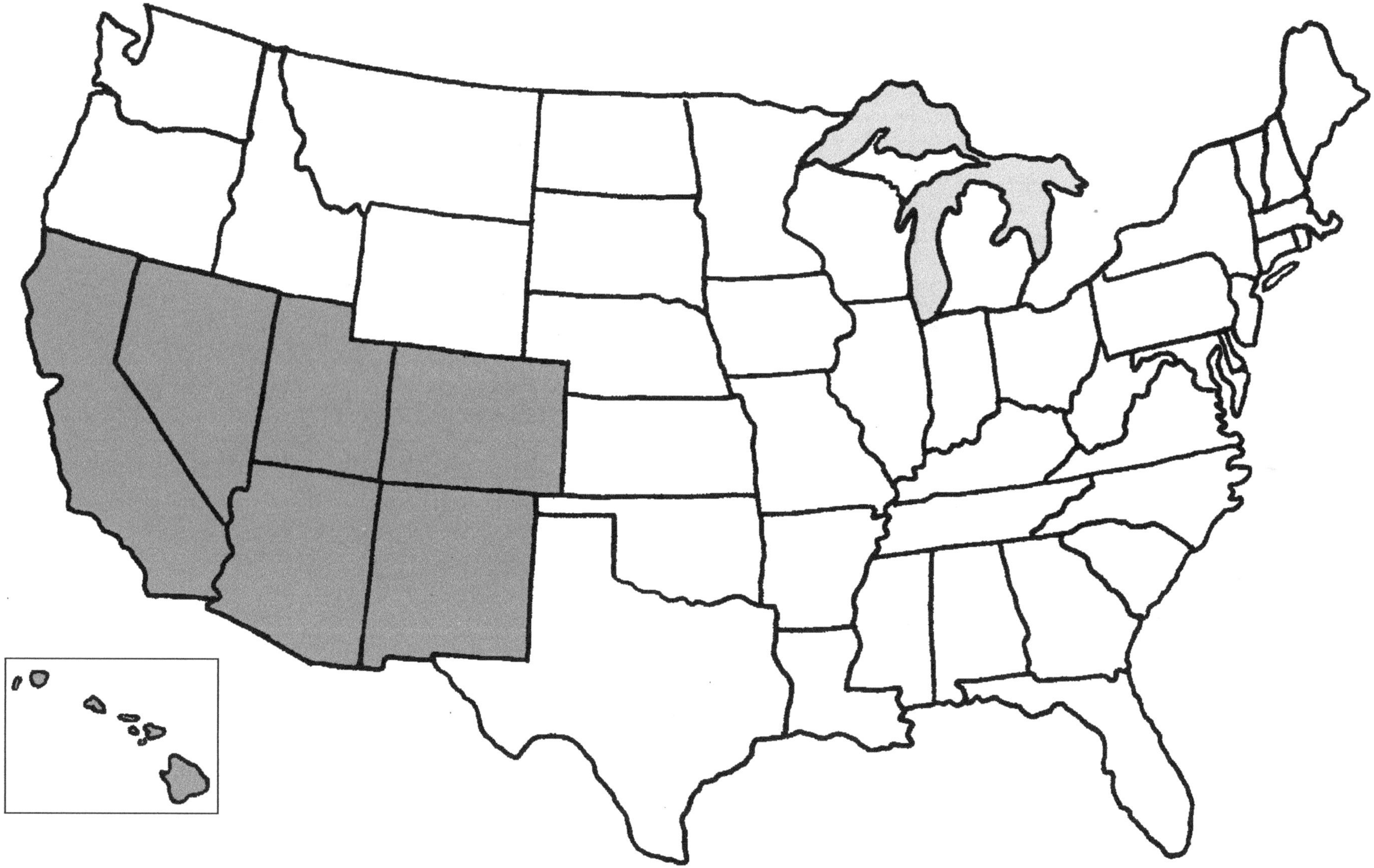

Copyright © 2016, Patricia Blackmer

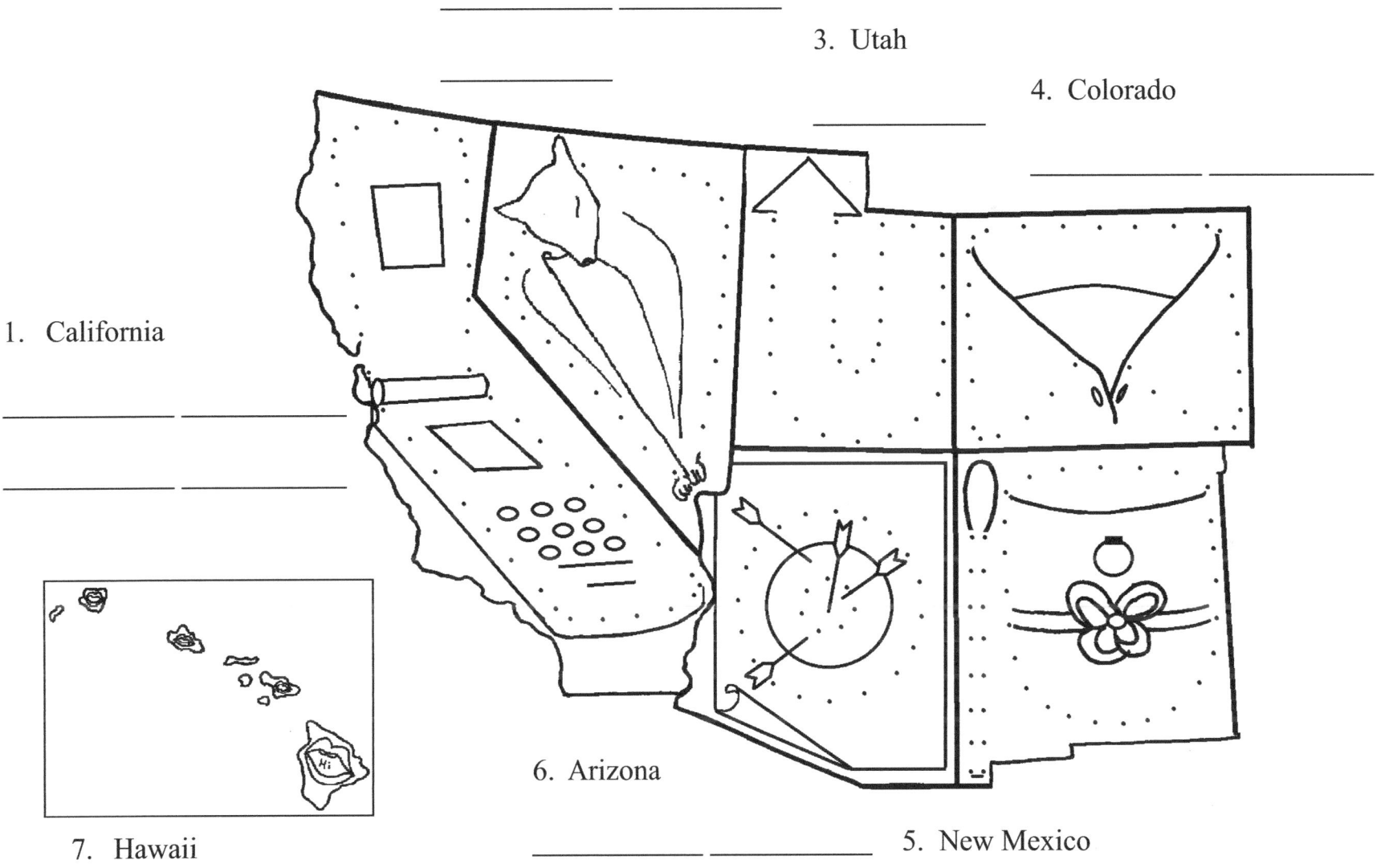

1. California
2. Nevada
3. Utah
4. Colorado
5. New Mexico
6. Arizona
7. Hawaii

One day I undertook a tour through the country, and the diversity and beauties of nature I met with in this charming season, expelled every gloomy and vexatious thought.

I can't say I was ever lost, but I was bewildered once for three days.

—Daniel Boone

CAPITALS

MAP 7: NORTHEASTERN CAPITALS

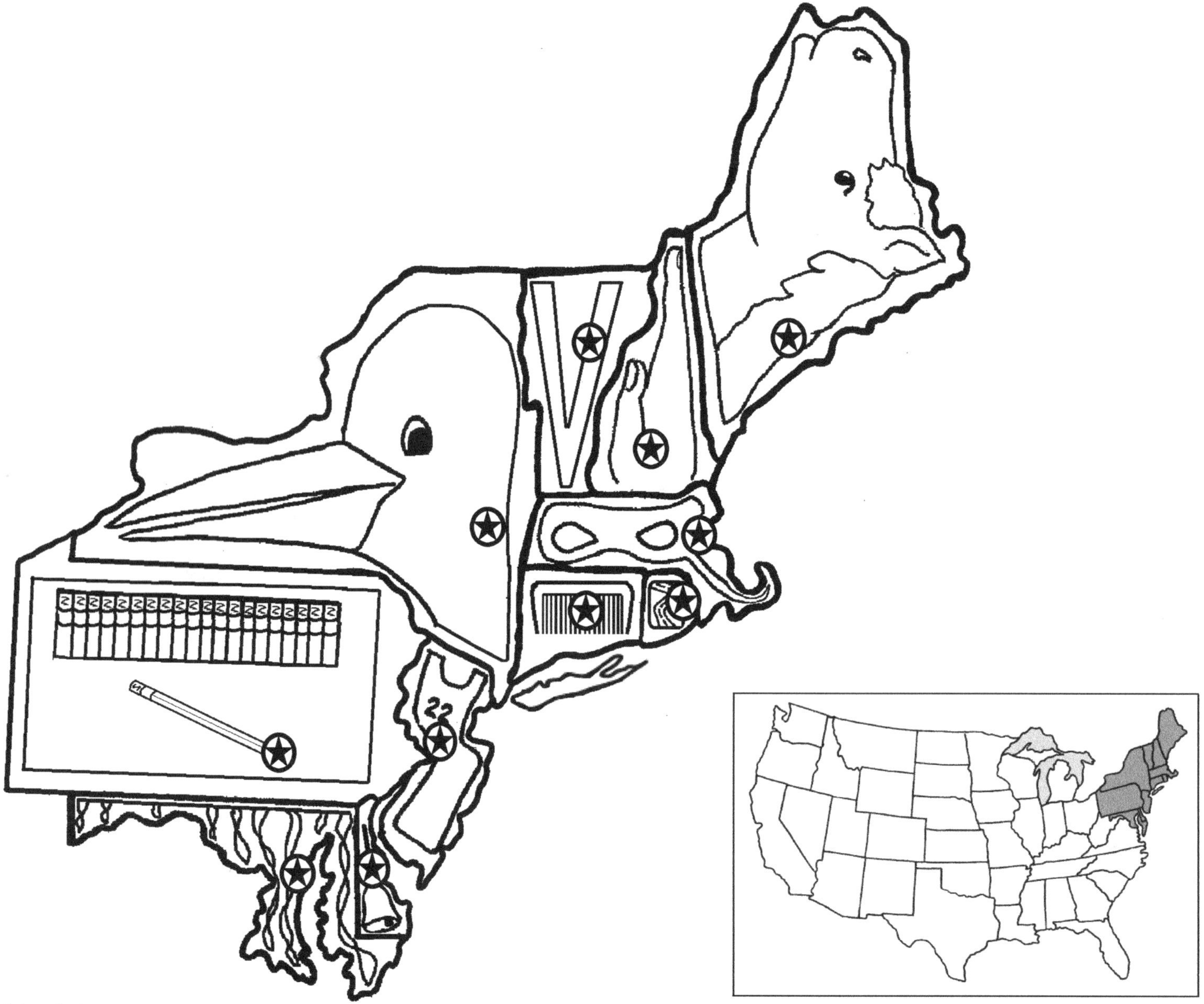

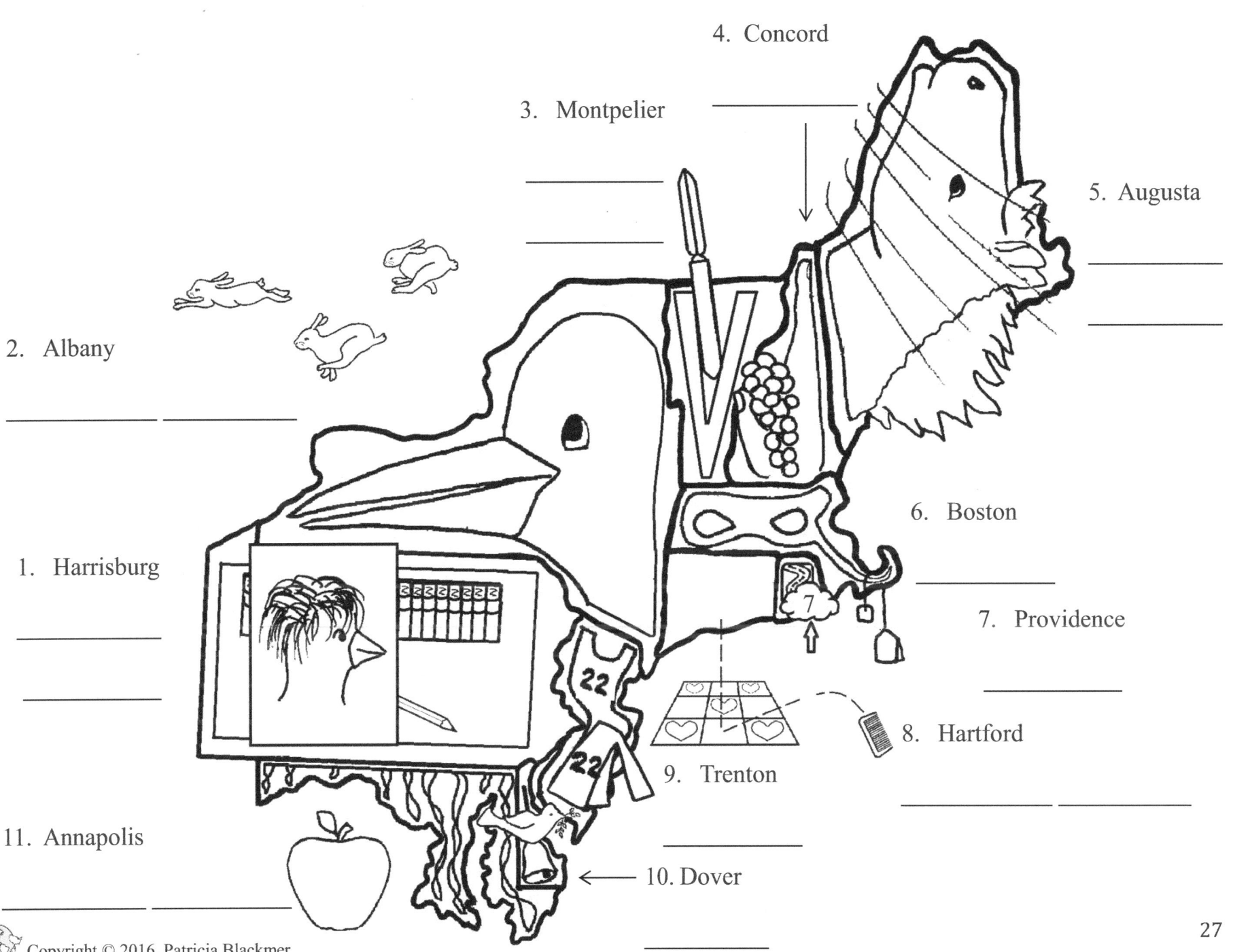

MAP 8: SOUTHEASTERN CAPITALS

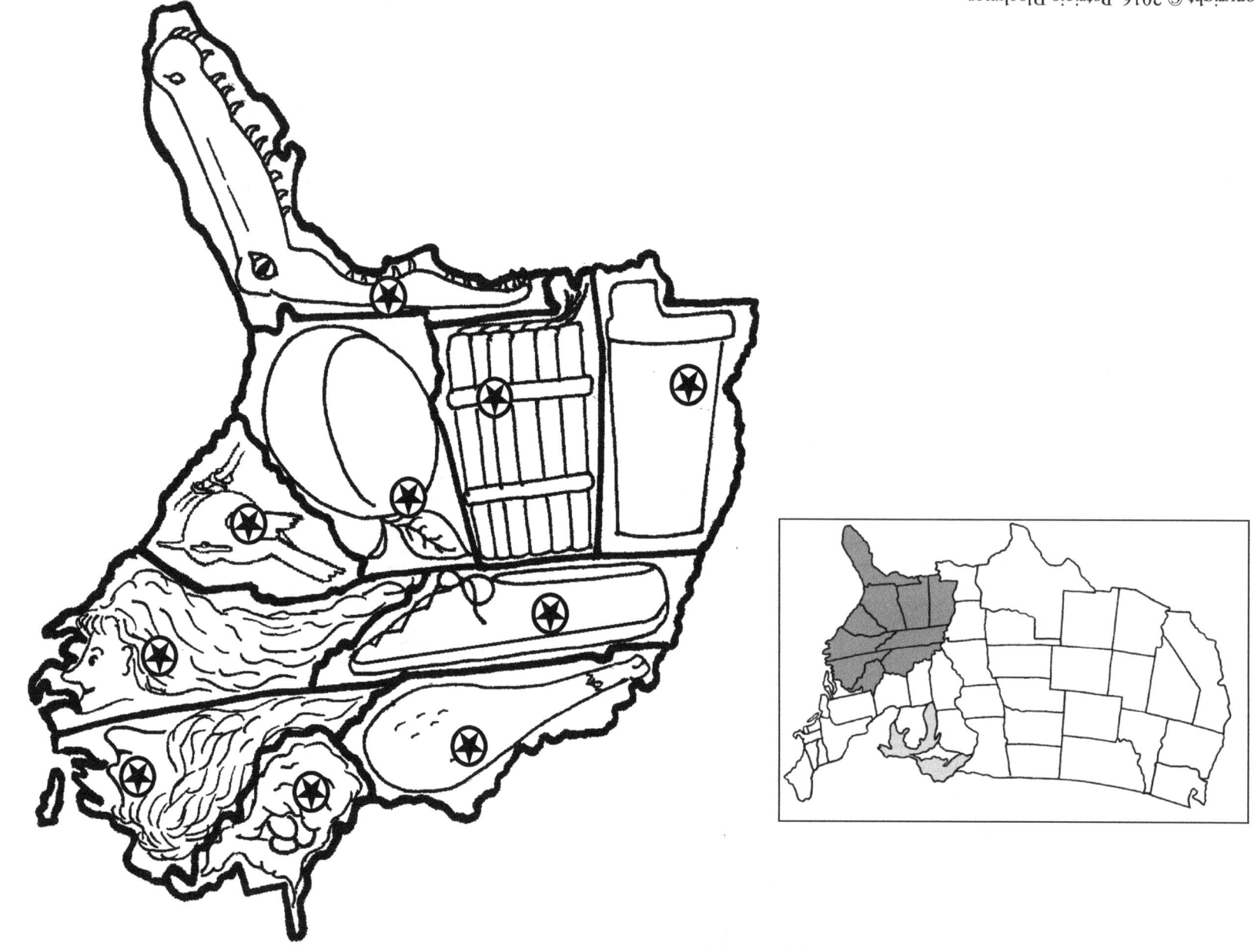

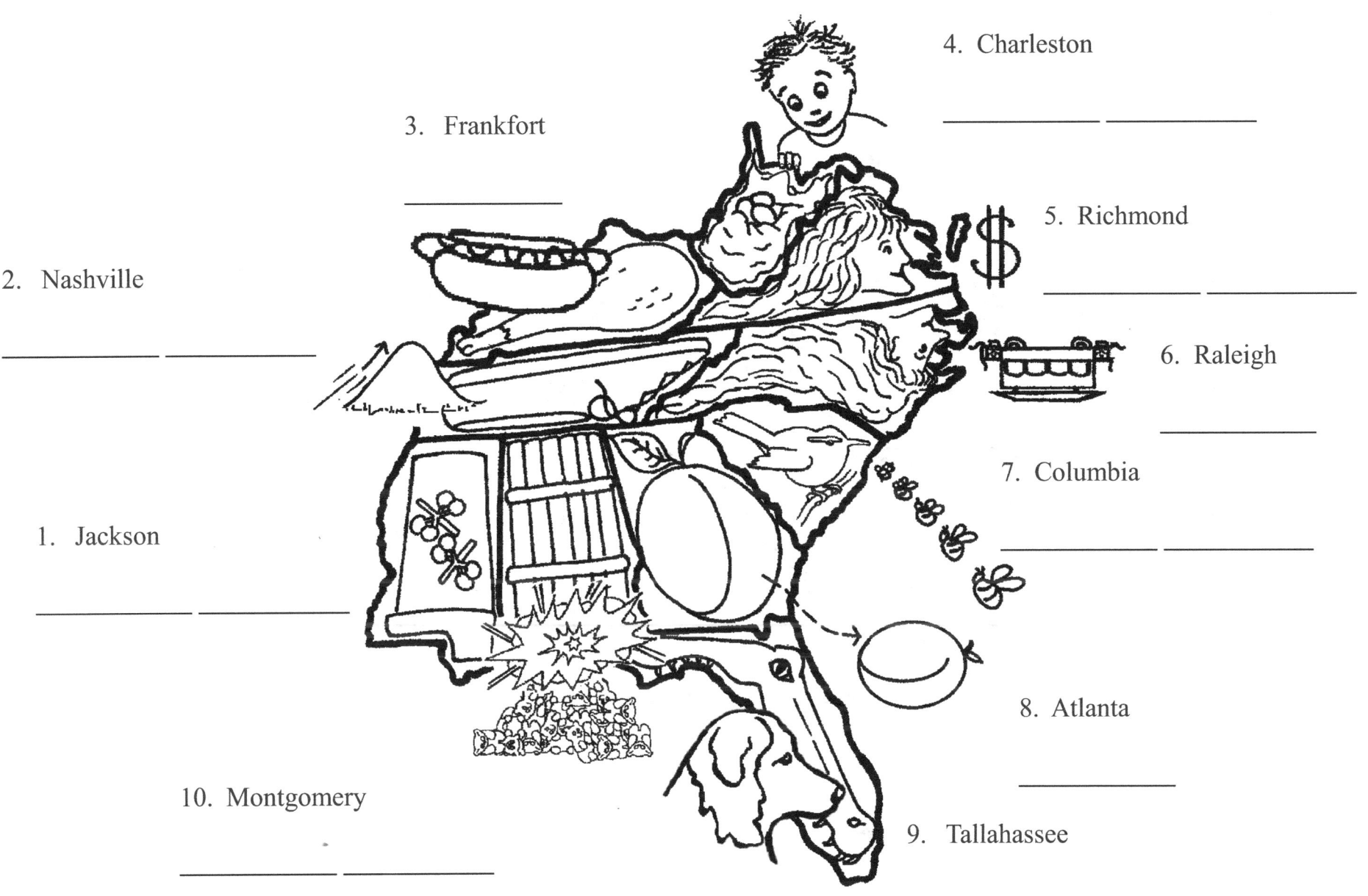

4. Charleston
3. Frankfort
5. Richmond
2. Nashville
6. Raleigh
7. Columbia
1. Jackson
8. Atlanta
9. Tallahassee
10. Montgomery

MAP 9: NORTH CENTRAL CAPITALS

30

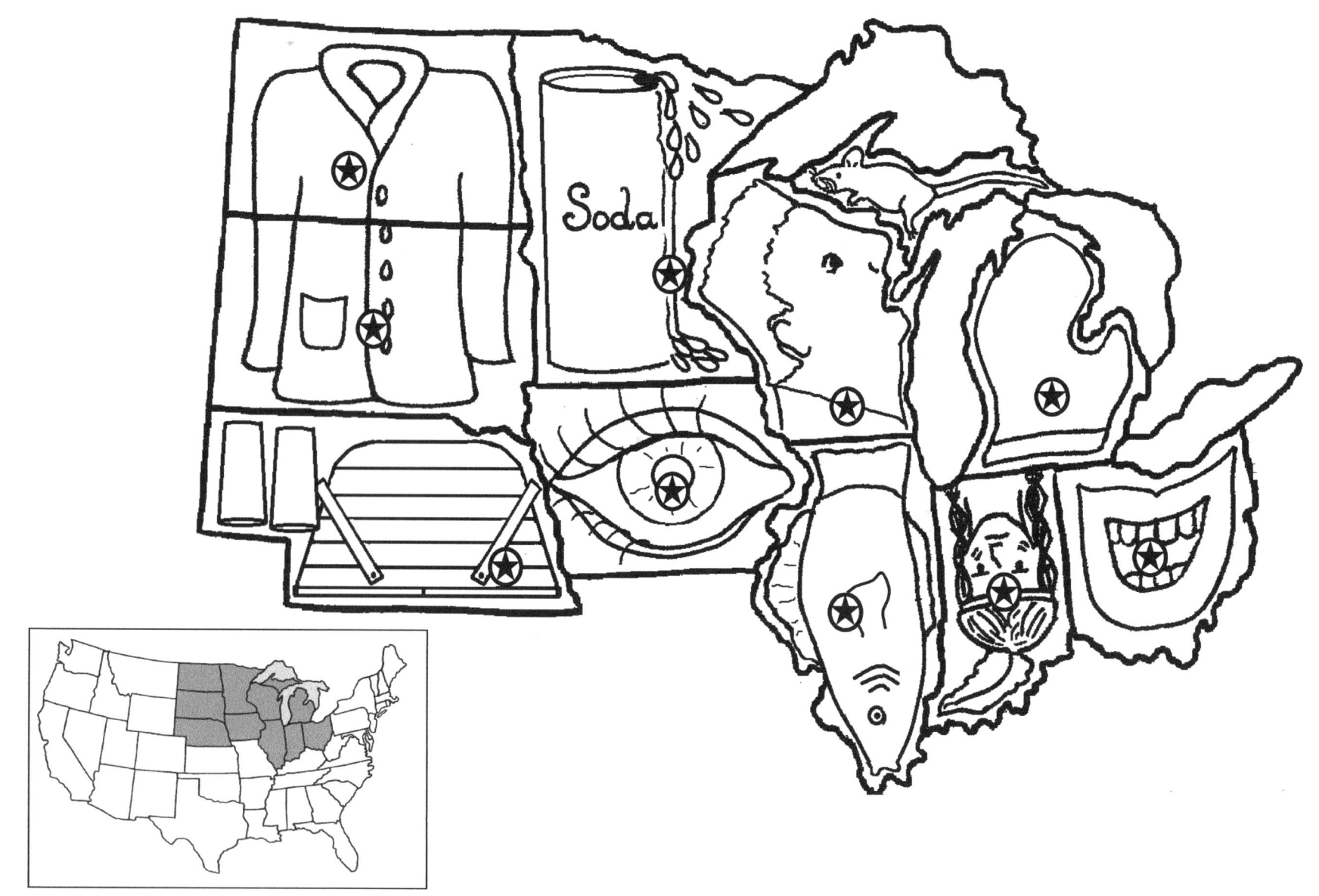

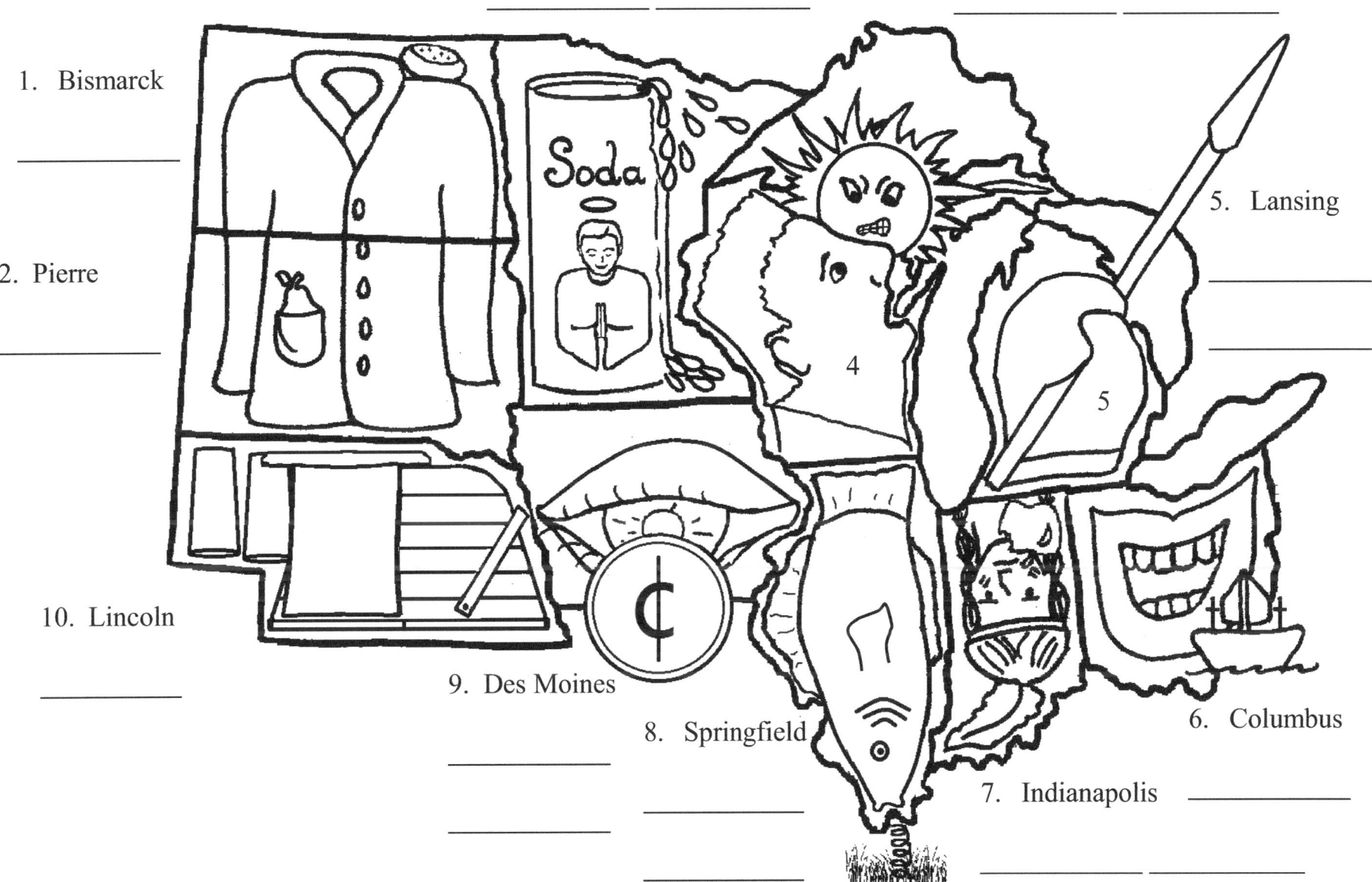

1. Bismarck
2. Pierre
3. Saint Paul
4. Madison
5. Lansing
6. Columbus
7. Indianapolis
8. Springfield
9. Des Moines
10. Lincoln

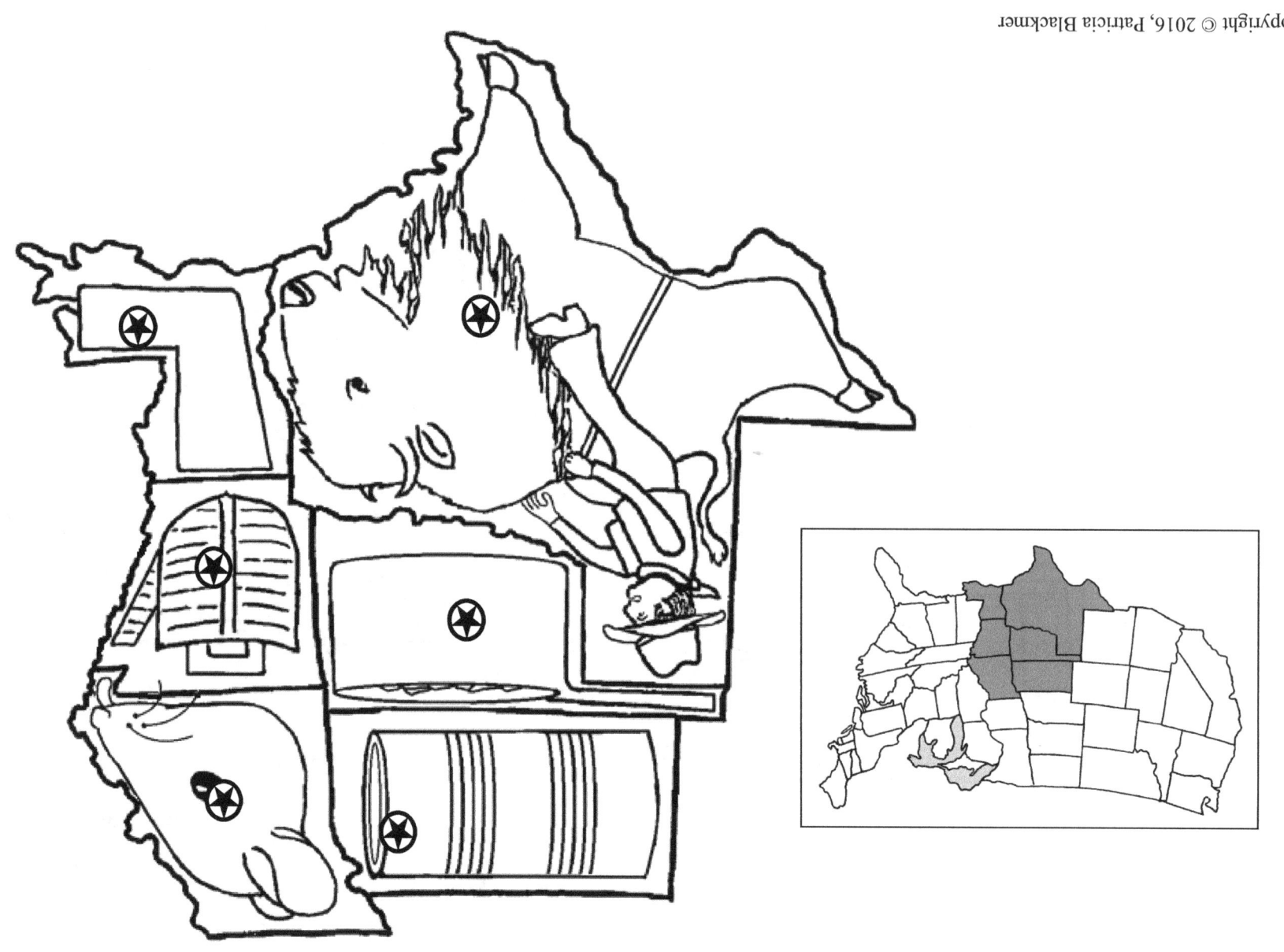

MAP 10: SOUTH CENTRAL CAPITALS

2. Topeka
_____ _____

3. Jefferson City
_____ _____

1. Oklahoma City
_____ _____

4. Little Rock
_____ _____

5. Baton Rouge
_____ _____

6. Austin
_____ _____

33

MAP 11: NORTHWESTERN CAPITALS

34

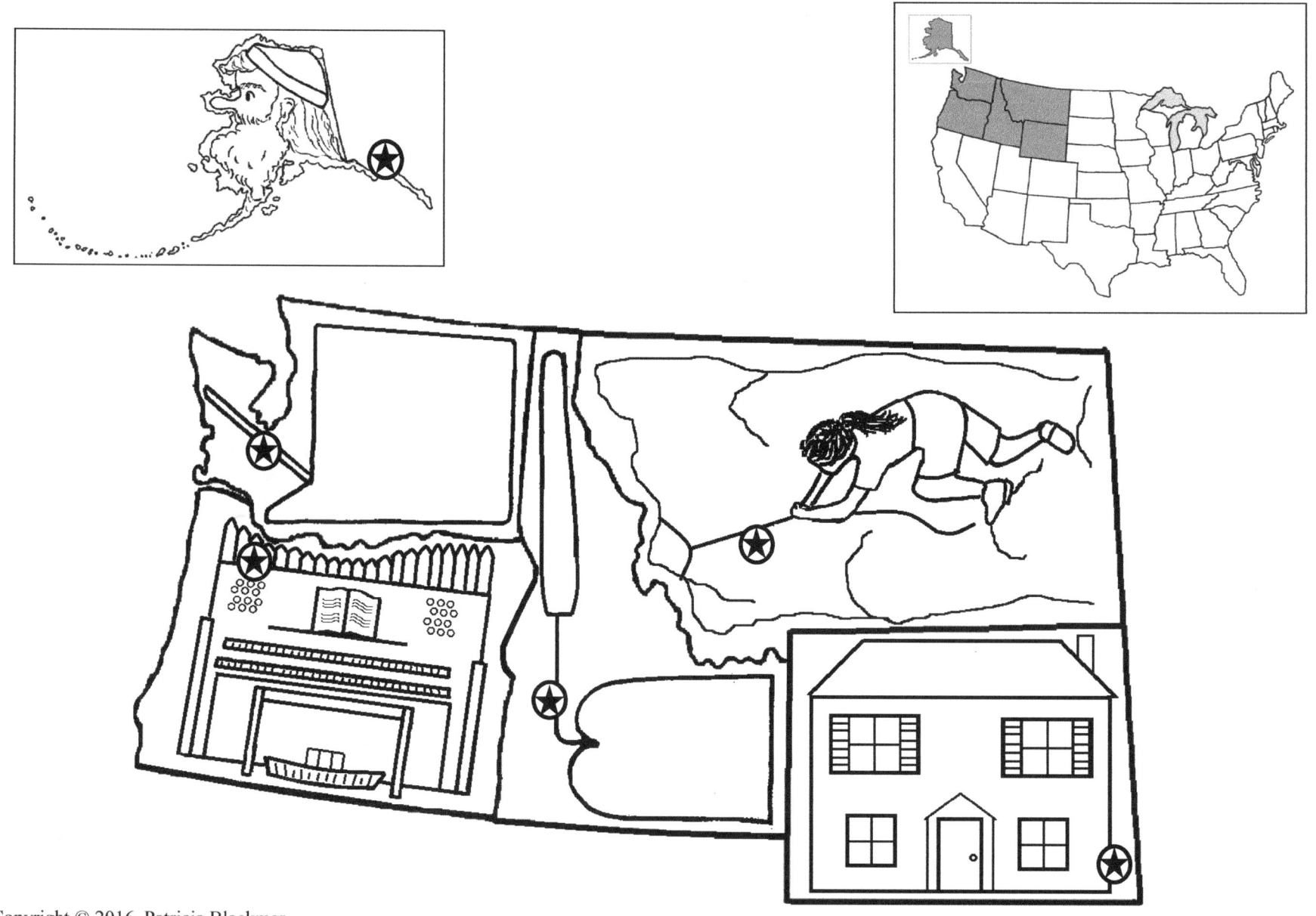

Copyright © 2016, Patricia Blackmer

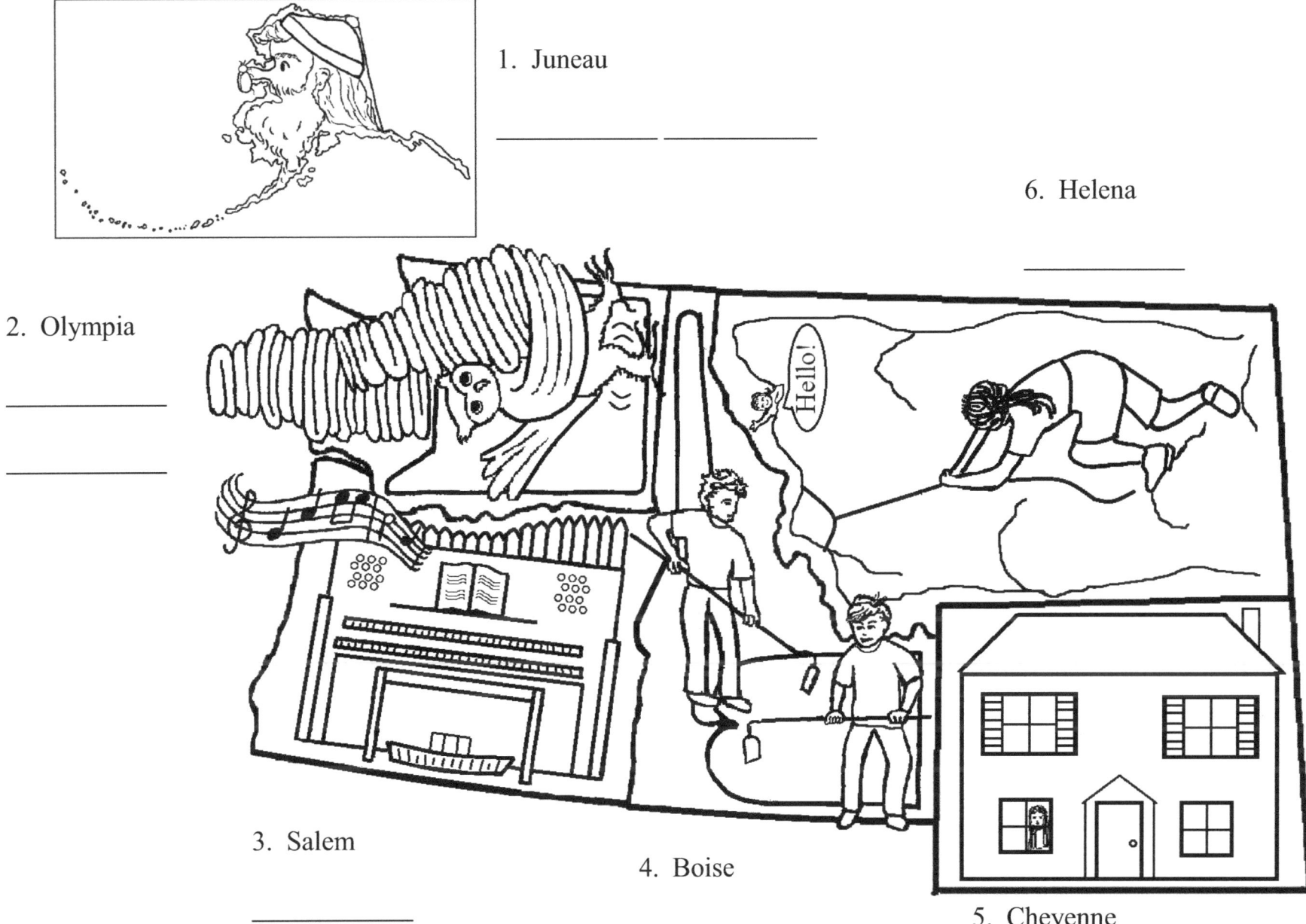

1. Juneau

_____ _____

6. Helena

_____

2. Olympia

_____

3. Salem

_____

4. Boise

_____

5. Cheyenne

_____ _____

Map 12: SOUTHWESTERN CAPITALS

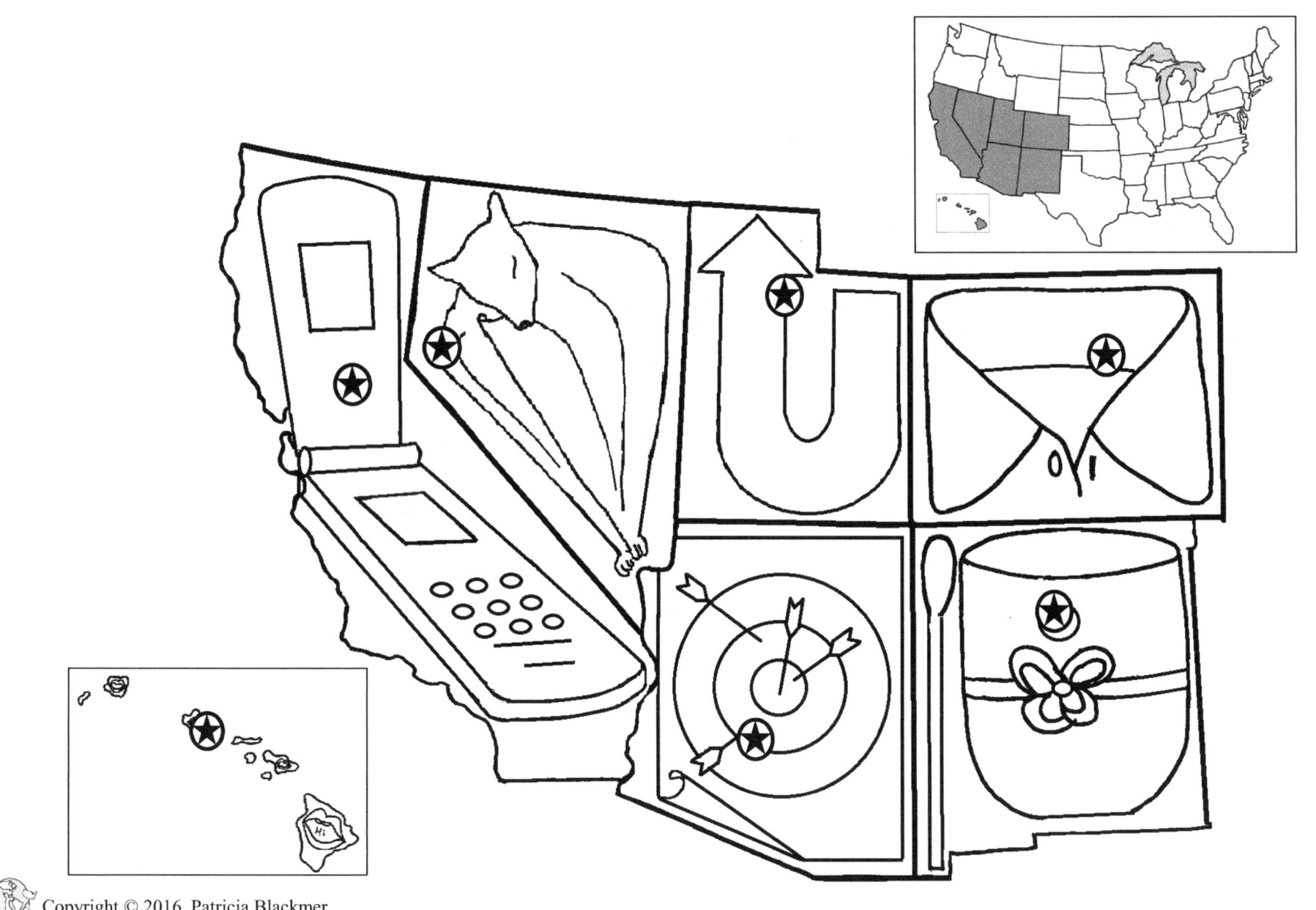

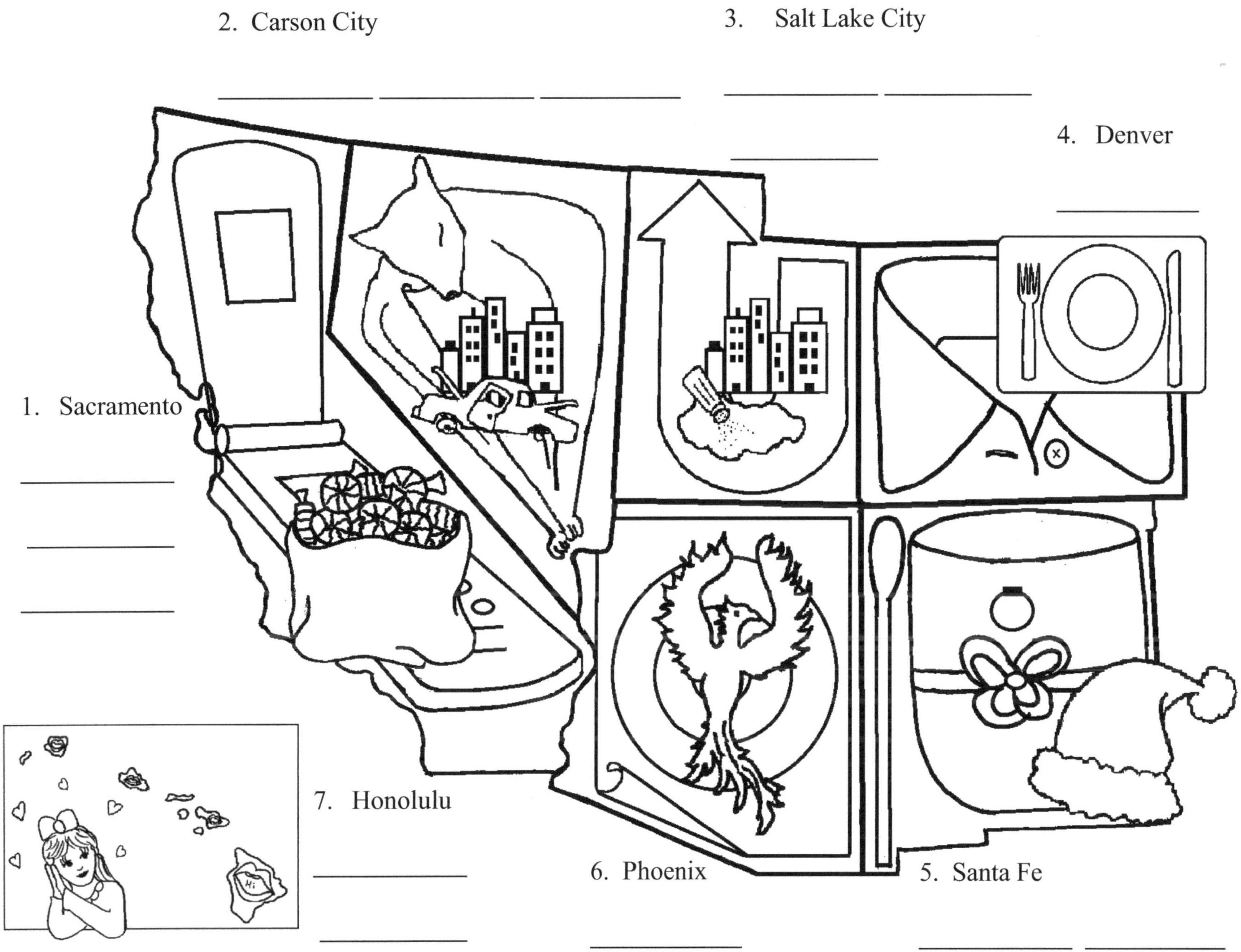

2. Carson City 3. Salt Lake City

4. Denver

1. Sacramento

7. Honolulu

6. Phoenix 5. Santa Fe

The face of the water, in time, became a wonderful book - a book that was a dead language
to the uneducated passenger, but which told its mind to me without reserve,
delivering its most cherished secrets as clearly as if it uttered them with a voice.
And it was not a book to be read once and thrown aside,
for it had a new story to tell every day.

—Mark Twain

PHYSICAL FEATURES

MAP 13: BODIES OF WATER

40

1. **Yukon** River: Al asks (Alaska) if _____ _____ drink as much water as he can.

2. **Columbia** River: She washed a ton (Washington) of clothes then folded them into _____.

3. **Snake** River: The _____ is coiled around Ida's hoe (Idaho).

4. **Great Salt** Lake: We made a U-turn (Utah) at the _____ _____.

5. **Colorado** River: Flows through _____.

6. **Rio Grande** River: It's _____ _____ because it separates two countries.

7. **Missouri** River: Flows through _____.

8. **Platte** River: There is a _____ in the picnic basket (Nebraska).

9. **Arkansas** River: Flows through _____.

10. **Red** River: The pot of okra at home (Oklahoma) is cooking on _____ hot coils.

11. **Mississippi** River: Flows west of _____.

12. **Ohio** River: Flows south of _____.

13. Lake **Superior**: A creature looking for his _____.

14. Lake **Michigan**: The other _____ that went though the wash.

15. Lake **Huron**: A _____ _____ the mitten.

16. Lake **Erie**: A rabbit's _____.

17. Lake **Ontario**: A _____ the rabbit's ear is listening to.

MAP 14: MOUNTAINS, DESERTS, PLAINS

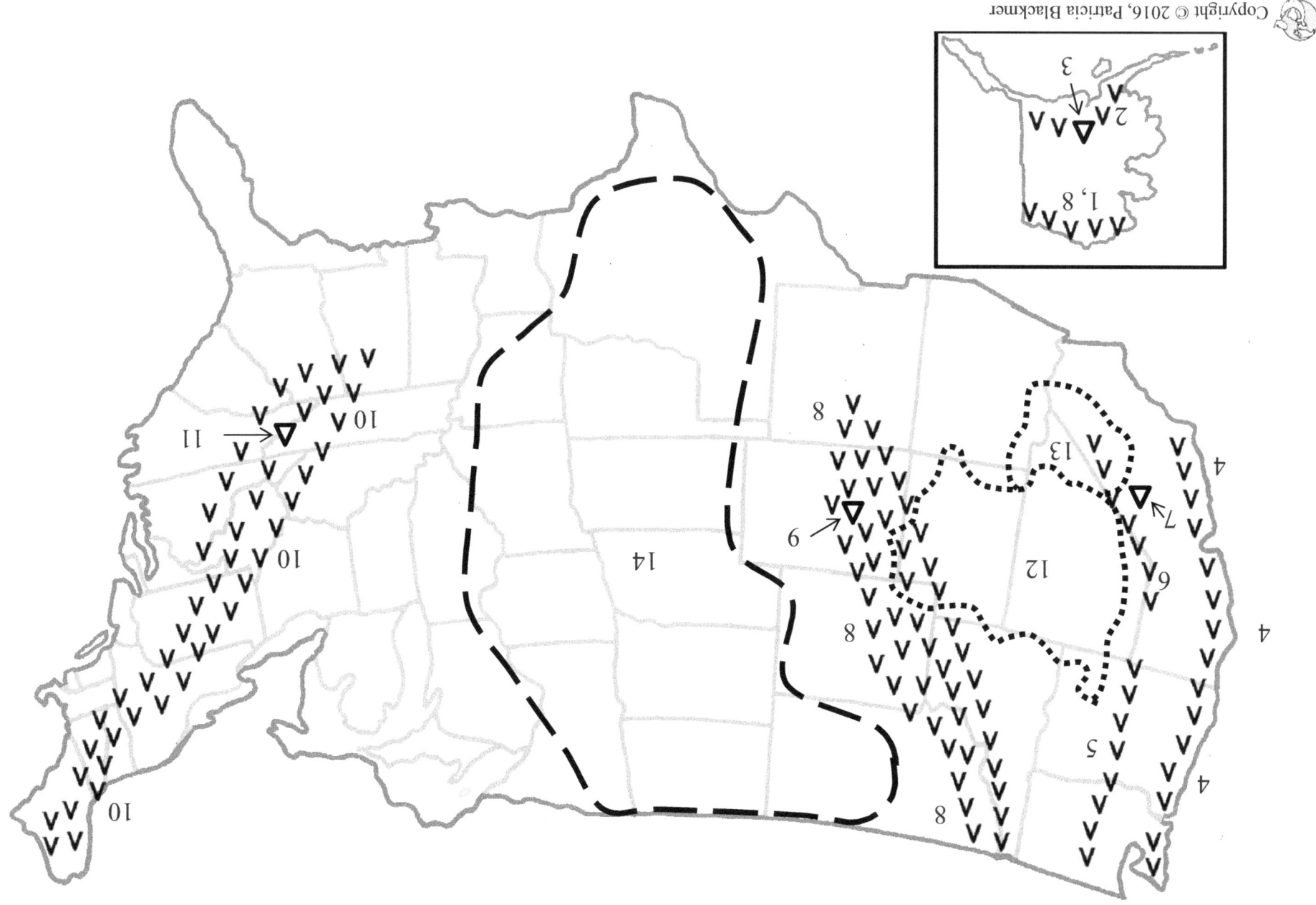

42

Mountains

1. **Brooks** Range: Al asks (Alaska) if he should wash his hair in the _____.

2. **Alaska** Range: In _____.

3. Mount **Denali (McKinley)**: Al asks (Alaska) who gave President _____ the _____.

4. **Coastal** Mountains: Run along the west _____.

5. **Cascade** Mountains: The water _____ down the washing machine (Washington).

6. **Sierra Nevada** Mountains: Touch _____.

7. Mount **Whitney**: He made the call on the phone (California) _____ _____.

8. **Rocky** Mountains: Al asks (Alaska) to store the _____ in the new mixing bowl (New Mexico).

9. Mount **Elbert**: _____ _____ he can wear the collar of Rod's (Colorado).

10. **Appalachian** Mountains: The horse with a mane (Maine) eats _____ and peaches (Georgia).

11. Mount **Mitchell**: Carolina (North Carolina) married _____.

Deserts

12. **Great Basin** Desert: The bat (Nevada) ate from the _____ _____.

13. **Mojave** Desert: The bat (Nevada) got a _____ haircut.

Plains

14. **Great** Plains: The _____ big _____ landed in the middle of the United States.

Copyright © 2016, Patricia Blackmer

While I viewed these mountains I felt a secret pleasure in finding myself so near the head of the heretofore conceived boundless Missouri; but when I reflected on the difficulties which this snowy barrier would most probably throw in my way to the Pacific, and the sufferings and hardships of myself and party in them, it in some measure counterbalanced the joy I had felt in the first moments in which I gazed on them; but as I have always held it a crime to anticipate evils I will believe it a good comfortable road until I am compelled to believe differently.

—The Journals of the Lewis and Clark Expedition

TESTS

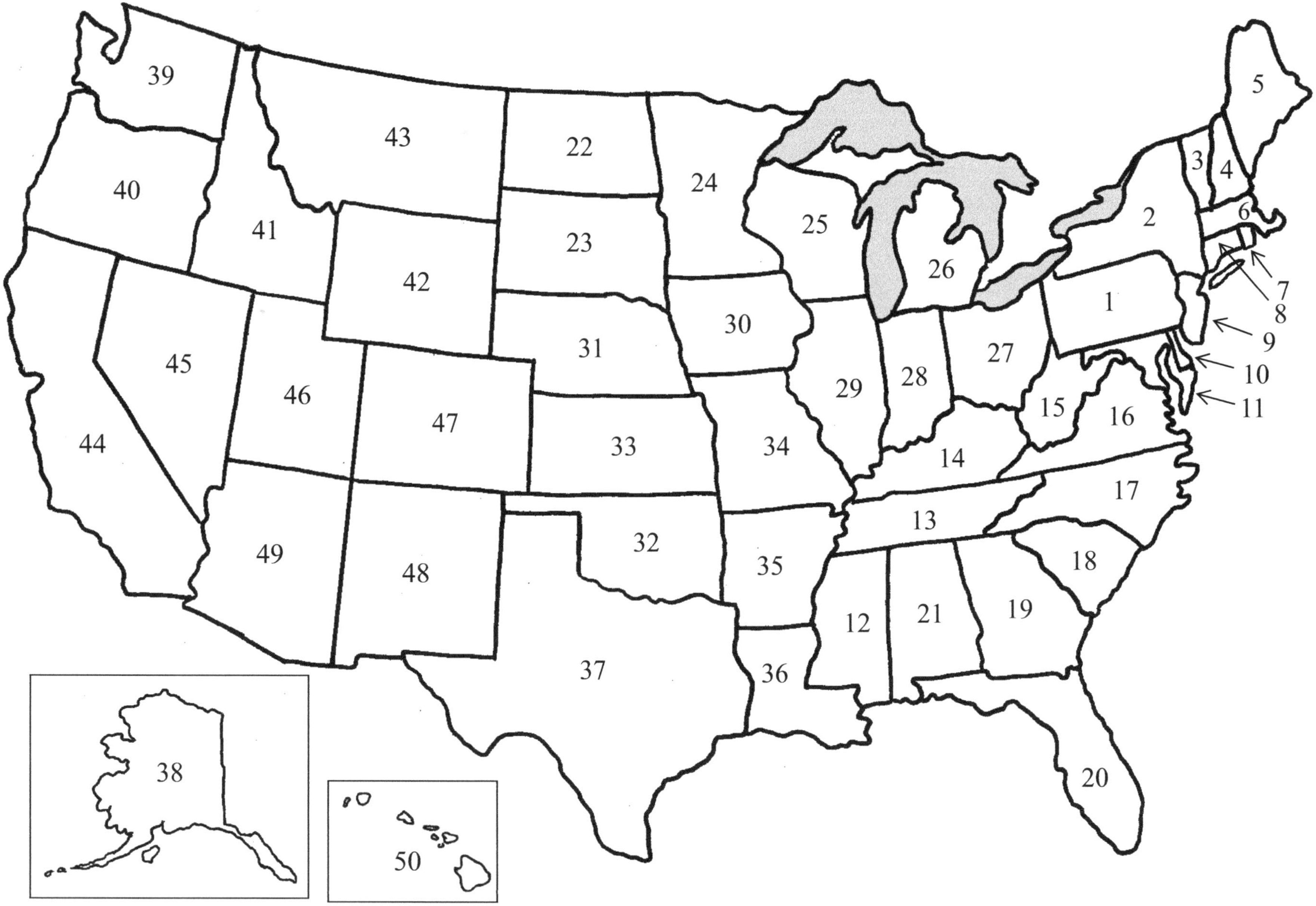

39
40
41
43
22
23
24
25
26
2
3
4
5
6
7
8
9
10
11
1
27
28
29
30
31
42
45
44
46
47
33
34
14
15
16
17
13
32
35
49
48
37
36
12
21
19
18
20
38
50

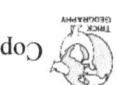

STATES

Match the correct state with its number on the page above.

1. _____	21. _____	41. _____	A.	Alabama	U.	Massachusetts	OO.	South Dakota
2. _____	22. _____	42. _____	B.	Alaska	V.	Michigan	PP.	Tennessee
3. _____	23. _____	43. _____	C.	Arizona	W.	Minnesota	QQ.	Texas
4. _____	24. _____	44. _____	D.	Arkansas	X.	Mississippi	RR.	Utah
5. _____	25. _____	45. _____	E.	California	Y.	Missouri	SS.	Vermont
6. _____	26. _____	46. _____	F.	Colorado	Z.	Montana	TT.	Virginia
7. _____	27. _____	47. _____	G.	Connecticut	AA.	Nebraska	UU.	Washington
8. _____	28. _____	48. _____	H.	Delaware	BB.	Nevada	VV.	West Virginia
9. _____	29. _____	49. _____	I.	Florida	CC.	New Hampshire	WW.	Wisconsin
10. _____	30. _____	50. _____	J.	Georgia	DD.	New Jersey	XX.	Wyoming
11. _____	31. _____		K.	Hawaii	EE.	New Mexico		
12. _____	32. _____		L.	Idaho	FF.	New York		
13. _____	33. _____		M.	Illinois	GG.	North Carolina		
14. _____	34. _____		N.	Indiana	HH.	North Dakota		
15. _____	35. _____		O.	Iowa	II.	Ohio		
16. _____	36. _____		P.	Kansas	JJ.	Oklahoma		
17. _____	37. _____		Q.	Kentucky	KK.	Oregon		
18. _____	38. _____		R.	Louisiana	LL.	Pennsylvania		
19. _____	39. _____		S.	Maine	MM.	Rhode Island		
20. _____	40. _____		T.	Maryland	NN.	South Carolina		

Copyright © 2016, Patricia Blackmer

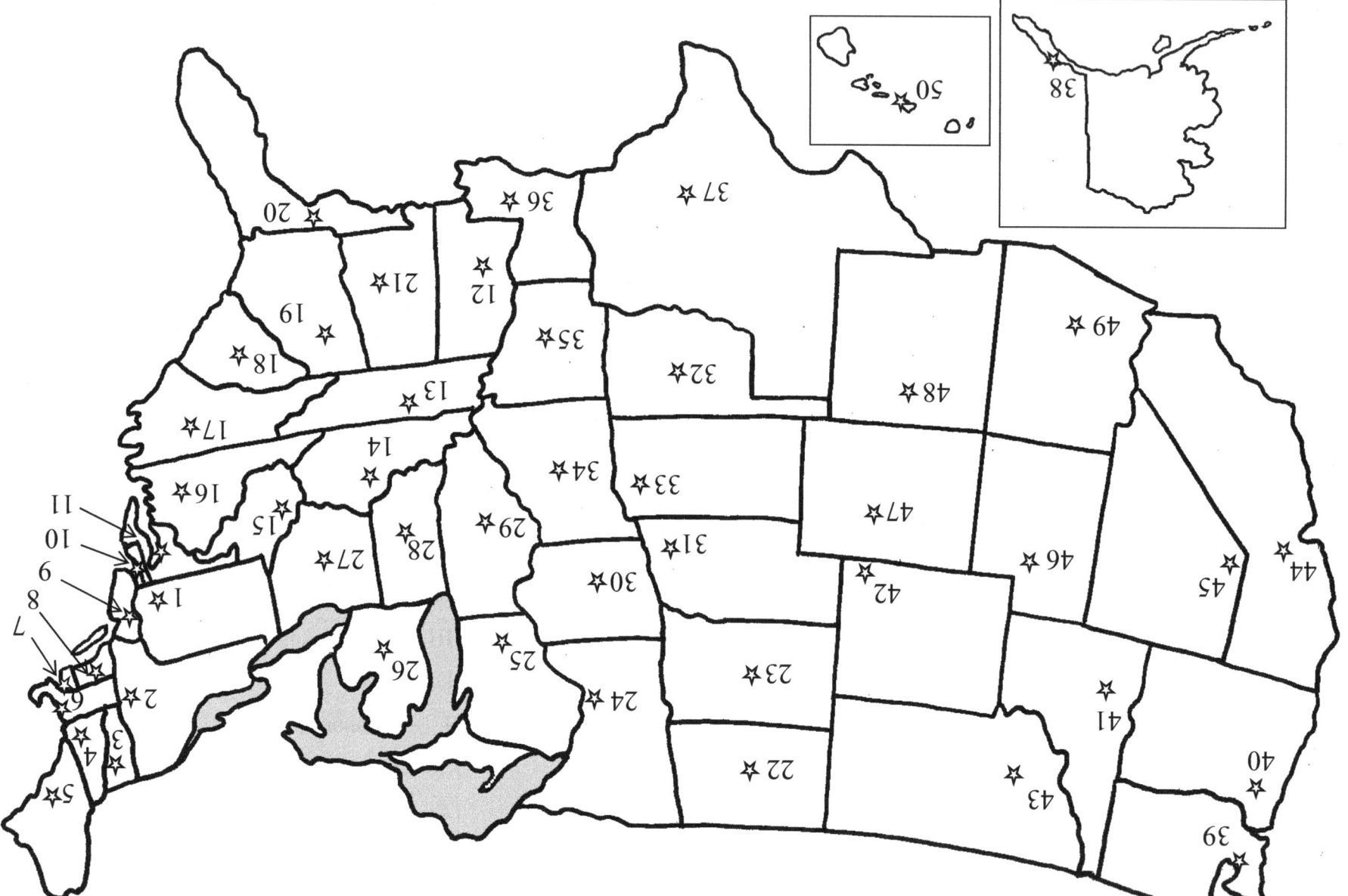

CAPITALS

Match the correct capital with its number on the page above.

1. ____	21. ____	41. ____	A.	Albany	U.	Hartford	OO.	Richmond
2. ____	22. ____	42. ____	B.	Annapolis	V.	Helena	PP.	Sacramento
3. ____	23. ____	43. ____	C.	Atlanta	W.	Honolulu	QQ.	St. Paul
4. ____	24. ____	44. ____	D.	Augusta	X.	Indianapolis	RR.	Salem
5. ____	25. ____	45. ____	E.	Austin	Y.	Jackson	SS.	Salt Lake City
6. ____	26. ____	46. ____	F.	Baton Rouge	Z.	Jefferson City	TT.	Santa Fe
7. ____	27. ____	47. ____	G.	Bismarck	AA.	Juneau	UU.	Springfield
8. ____	28. ____	48. ____	H.	Boise	BB.	Lansing	VV.	Tallahassee
9. ____	29. ____	49. ____	I.	Boston	CC.	Lincoln	WW.	Topeka
10. ____	30. ____	50. ____	J.	Carson City	DD.	Little Rock	XX.	Trenton
11. ____	31. ____		K.	Charleston	EE.	Madison		
12. ____	32. ____		L.	Cheyenne	FF.	Montgomery		
13. ____	33. ____		M.	Columbia	GG.	Montpelier		
14. ____	34. ____		N.	Columbus	HH.	Nashville		
15. ____	35. ____		O.	Concord	II.	Oklahoma City		
16. ____	36. ____		P.	Denver	JJ.	Olympia		
17. ____	37. ____		Q.	Des Moines	KK.	Phoenix		
18. ____	38. ____		R.	Dover	LL.	Pierre		
19. ____	39. ____		S.	Frankfort	MM.	Providence		
20. ____	40. ____		T.	Harrisburg	NN.	Raleigh		

Copyright © 2016, Patricia Blackmer

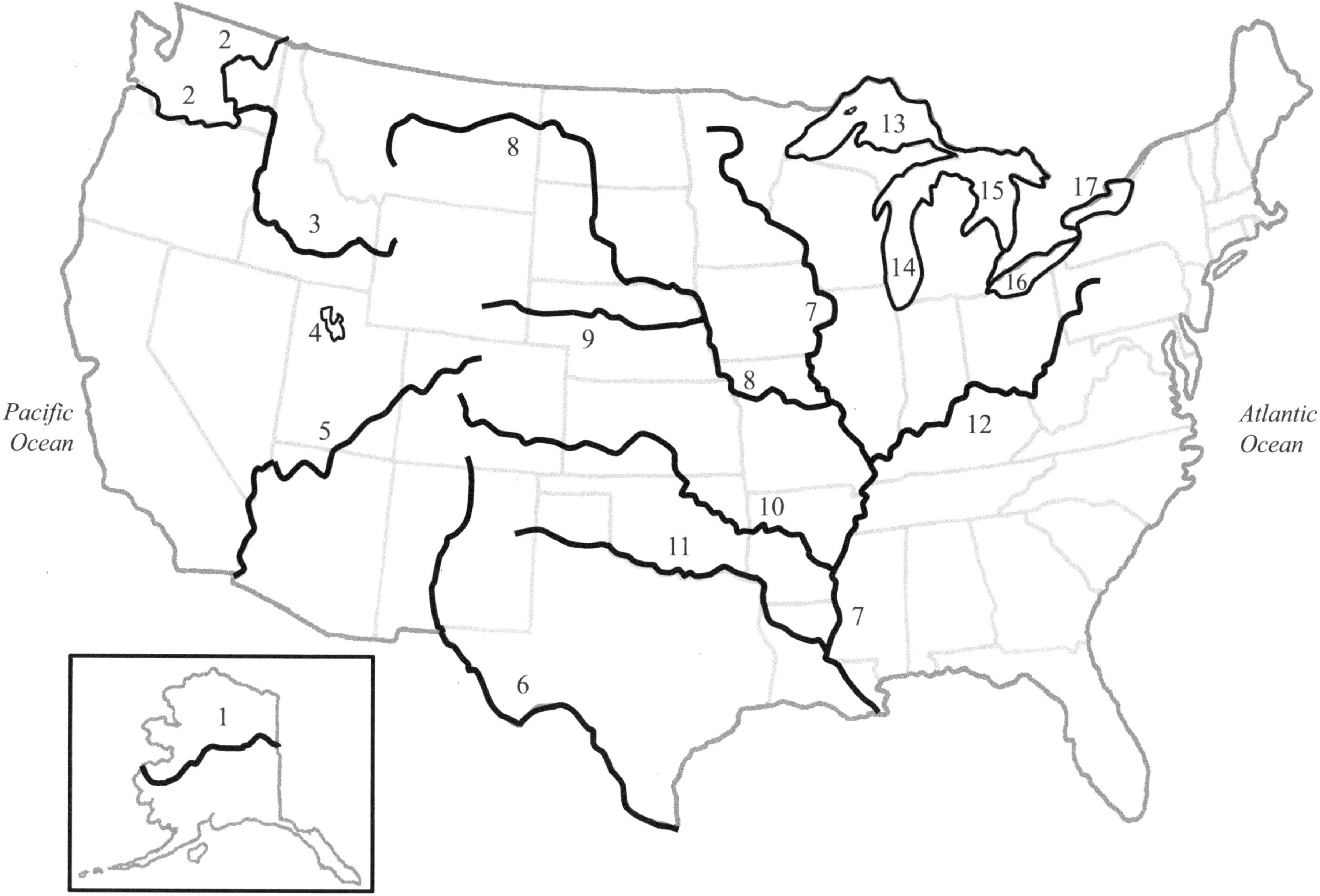

2
2
3
4
5
8
9
8
7
6
10
11
7
12
13
14
15
16
17
Pacific Ocean
Atlantic Ocean
1

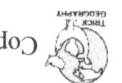

BODIES OF WATER

Match the correct body of water with its number on the page above.

1. _____
2. _____
3. _____
4. _____
5. _____
6. _____
7. _____
8. _____
9. _____
10. _____
11. _____
12. _____
13. _____
14. _____
15. _____
16. _____
17. _____

A. Arkansas
B. Colorado
C. Columbia
D. Erie
E. Great Salt
F. Huron
G. Michigan
H. Mississippi
I. Missouri
J. Ohio
K. Ontario
L. Platte
M. Red
N. Rio Grande
O. Snake
P. Superior
Q. Yukon

Copyright © 2016, Patricia Blackmer

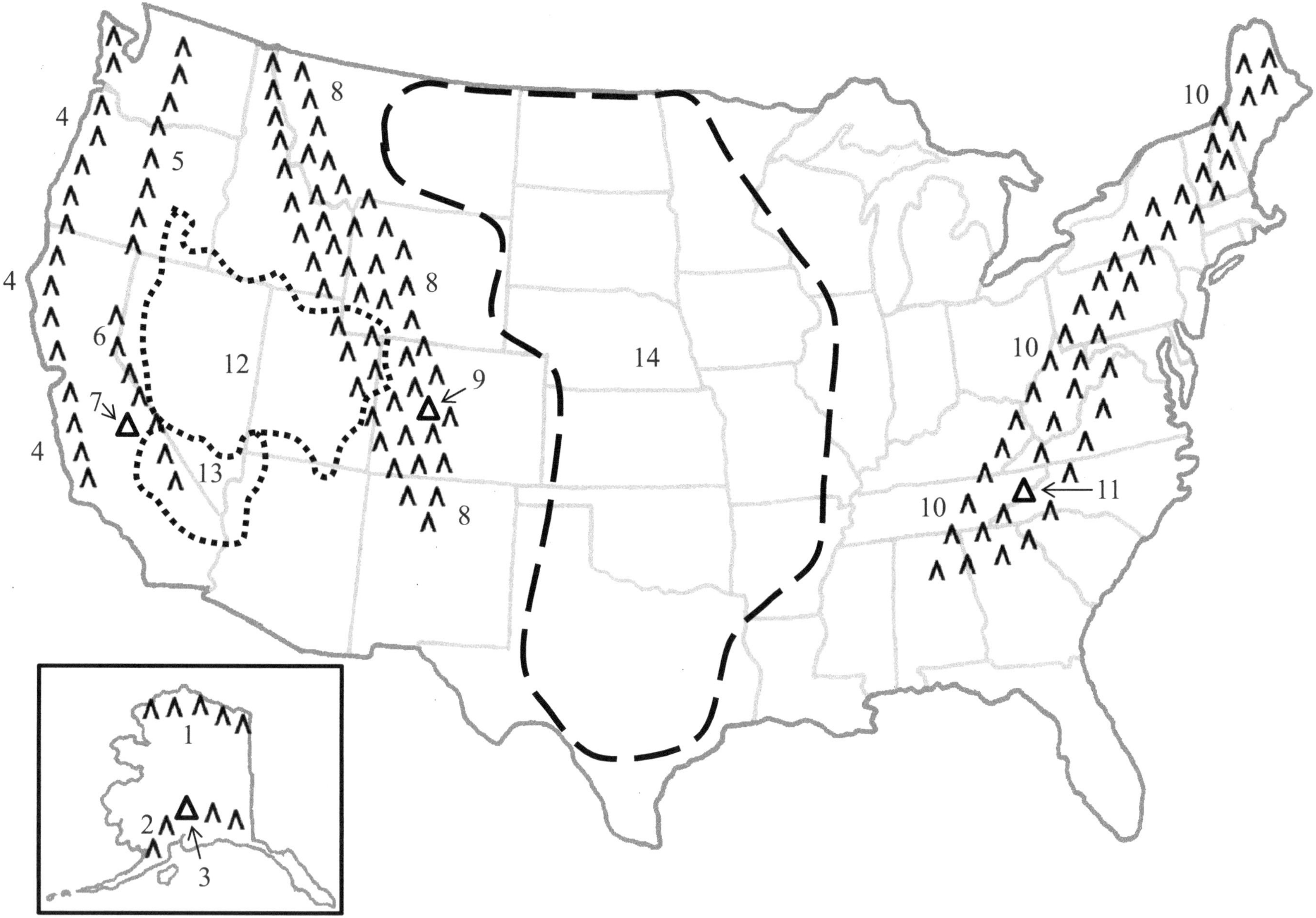
10
4
8
5
4
8
6
12
14
10
9
7
11
4
13
10
8
1
2
3

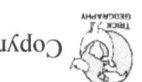

MOUNTAINS, DESERTS, PLAINS

Match the correct mountain, desert, or plain with its number on the page above.

1. _____
2. _____
3. _____
4. _____
5. _____
6. _____
7. _____
8. _____
9. _____
10. _____
11. _____
12. _____
13. _____
14. _____

A. Alaska
B. Appalachian
C. Brooks
D. Cascade
E. Coastal
F. Denali (McKinley)
G. Elbert
H. Great Basin
I. Great Plains
J. Mitchell
K. Mojave
L. Rocky
M. Sierra Nevada
N. Whitney

God bless America, land that I love.
Stand beside her, and guide her
Through the night with the light from above.
From the mountains, to the prairies,
To the oceans white with foam,
God bless America, my home sweet home.

—Irving Berlin

Where do we go from here?

I hope you have enjoyed learning US geography with *Trick Geography: USA*. But this is only the beginning. You have been given lots of hooks on which to hang lots of information.

Now you can come up with your own tricks to learn additional US **cities**, **islands**, **rivers**, **lakes**, **mountains**, **deserts**, **plains**, or other **places** in the United States you wish to remember. You might say, "*My home* (Wyoming) is built out of *yellow stones* (Yellowstone National Park)."

You'll find yourself more connected to the world around you—just because you know where places are. The **news** will catch your attention when you hear about an **event** that just happened in a place you recognize now. You will know that a dramatic freighter rescue in Lake Ontario took place in the *stereo*. A **weather** report about tornados in Oklahoma will trigger an image of a pot of *okra* cooking at *home* and your radar will quickly hone in on the south central United States.

Use what you've learned to help you in **history**. Do you know where George Washington fought the battle of Valley Forge? Pennsylvania. Can you come up with a way to remember that? Perhaps you might think, "Washington's soldiers drew pictures of the *valley* with *pencils*."

You can hang facts about famous **people** on your mental hooks, too. Where did Daniel Boone do his exploring? You could say, "*Daniel Boone* ate *Ken's turkey* leg on his explore." Now do you know?

A friend's **account** of her vacation to Sacramento will mean a little more to you now. And you'll know where those beautiful Coastal Mountains are that she drove along.

You get the picture. There are lots of ways to use *Trick Geography: USA* beyond simply knowing your map better. I hope you're able to use them. Thanks for coming along!

Perhaps you'd enjoy learning the entire world with *Trick Geography: World*.

See you there!

Patty Blackmer

TRICK GEOGRAPHY®
Companion Series
The quick and simple way to geographic mastery!

"I can't believe how much I just learned!" That was one mom's response after observing a single class session of *Trick Geography*.

Trick Geography routinely moves students from geographic illiteracy to command of world countries and US states with ease and high retention. It also teaches world and US capitals and major bodies of water, mountains, peninsulas, and deserts.

Delightful graphics, phonetic connectors, dot-to-dots, and fill-in-the-blanks facilitate multiple learning styles. The process is more like a game than a curriculum. While *Trick Geography* is easy enough for elementary students, it is sophisticated enough for the high schooler.

Teachers appreciate the simple instructions which require virtually no prep time and which give students the option of going through the program on their own. Pronunciation guides for many names expedite the teaching process as well.

Evaluation is a cinch with matching tests.

Trick Geography: USA

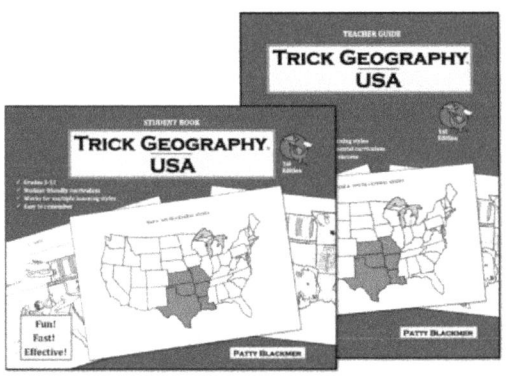

Trick Geography: World

Contact Trick Geography for quantity discounts at:
TrickGeography@outlook.com